DOG STORIES
with Happy Endings

To, Sharron + Kate,
Love + Best
Wishes!

Connie
Newcomb

DOG STORIES

with Happy Endings

CONNIE NEWCOMB

With contributions from Chris Iliades,
Corinne Iliades Sheh, and Jennifer Smith Iliades

"If my dog doesn't like you, I probably won't either!"
—Anonymous

"A dog is the only animal on earth that will love you more than he loves himself."
—Josh Billing

"Love me, love my dog."
—Anonymous

"Happiness is a warm puppy."
—Charles M. Schulz

"If there are no dogs in heaven, then when I die, I want to go where they went."
—Will Rogers

"There is always room for one more dog."
—Anonymous
(I think I may also have said that one!)

For Jack, the happiest dog I have ever known.

ACKNOWLEDGMENTS

THIS IS A COLLECTION OF TRUE STORIES about the dogs of childhood and adulthood owned by myself, friends, and family. Thanks to all who shared their memories. Special thanks to Chris Iliades, my brother; his wife, Karen; and their children, Nick, Tina, and Corinne, along with Jenn, Nick's wife, for sharing recollections of their pets, past and present.

I could not have created this book without the help of some other wonderful people. Many thanks to my editors Wendy Herlich, Alice Peck, and Jan Hooker-Haring. And to my cover designer Duane Stapp.

TABLE OF CONTENTS

Back in the Day 1

Yo, Rinny! 11

A Dog Named Piccolo. 19

Not a Dog Story (The Era of Cats) 27

Kenya, the Lion Dog. 35

Our Firstborn Child Had Fur 41

Two Greyhounds. 55

The Real Dogs of Princeton Court 61

Only the Good Die Young. 71

Garcia 75

The Wizard of Food 87

Niko. 91

Harper. 95

Carl and the Gang. 101

The Excellent Adventures of Bill and Ted. 113

I Don't Want Any More Dogs! 119

The Lovely Miss Ella. 129

Terra 137

Covered in Dogs 143

INTRODUCTION

DOGS MARK TIME IN OUR LIVES: when we were children, teenagers, and young adults going off to college, or perhaps when we were first married and having children. If you were lucky enough to have one, you will always remember a dog as part of your family. The memories of our pets conjure up specific details from times when our beloved companions were always there. When I think of Simon, my first dog as a grown-up, I see him playing in our backyard with my two young toddlers. I can picture my daughter's curly auburn hair blowing in the summer breeze as Simon chased her, and I can hear my son's laughter filling the air as he tried to keep up. Simon was their protector and my best friend. Every early family photo includes our first family dog. He inspired the deep love of animals felt by my children, who are now in their twenties, making special memories with dogs of their own.

This memoir focuses on pet stories with happy endings, which are sure to bring on a smile! Most of our pets were far from perfect, but all were very special. So cuddle up with your dog or cat (our family cats also make some appearances in this book) and get ready to reminisce about your own wonderful animals. I guarantee you will see a little bit of yourself and your pet in a story or two!

Back in the Day

THE DOGS OF OUR YOUTH seem to grow in legend, becoming more idealized as we age. "Remember old Buster? He was such a smart dog," or "Wasn't Chip a good boy? He was the best!" someone might remark at a family gathering. When my brother and I talk about our first dog, we agree that there never was a dog as wonderful as our Rin Tin Tin.

My love of dogs was handed down from my father's side of the family. As far as I know, my mother never had a dog as a child. Dad, however, often spoke of his beloved pets, usually with tears in his eyes. He always owned a dog or two, mostly strays, as had his father before him. One of the only photos I have of my grandfather shows him with my grandmother on an outing with the family dog. It was taken sometime before World War II in Greece. It's a photo I treasure, since my grandparents look quite happy to be out for a walk with their beloved pet.

My father's favorite dog as a child was Vero, a little mutt who went everywhere with him. Little Vero passed away when Dad was a teenager, but according to my father, there was never a more perfect pooch. Sadly, Dad also passed away many years ago, and stories of Vero have faded from our memories. But the dogs of my childhood are still quite vivid in my mind, from a time when life seemed to be so simple and our dogs were there to share in the fun.

I grew up during the sixties in a sleepy little town in northern New Jersey called Cedar Grove. At that time it was a place where there were still farms and plenty of woods. We lived in a neighborhood where everyone knew each other and there were lots of kids and dogs with whom to play.

Some of my first memories involve a large, handsome German shepherd guarding my crib. Did this really happen? I don't know. It may just be a legend that was created long ago. Regardless, Rin Tin Tin, or "Rinny" as we called him, was certainly an excellent dog.

My brother, Chris, was six years older than I. Rin Tin Tin was still a puppy when I was born. He was my brother's dog and constant companion. They were inseparable and created a perfect picture—like something out of a Norman Rockwell painting.

Rinny was very clever. One of my first clear memories of him is from Chris's tenth birthday party. I was sitting on our wooden picnic bench on the back patio, four years old and feeling quite pretty in my pink party dress. Chris's friends were settling down for some birthday cake. They had just finished playing Pin the Tail on the Donkey. I was petting Rinny's head, waiting patiently.

Finally, we sang "Happy Birthday," Chris blew out the candles, and Mom began to serve the delicious-looking cake. Rinny especially loved sweets. He carefully picked out an unsuspecting child (I think his name was John) and approached him silently. As soon as John's back was turned, Rinny snatched the entire piece off his plate and gobbled it down, so quickly that no one was the wiser. Before he trotted away happily, he gave me a look. He knew I had seen him, and he knew I wouldn't tell. Poor John had no clue what had happened to his cake. He simply stared down at his plate, looking quite surprised in his party hat and plaid shirt. Mom quickly got him another piece and put Rinny in the house.

Rinny loved to dig very big holes and put things into them. (I can remember spraining my ankle in one of those holes.) He enjoyed stealing objects of interest and burying them for safekeeping.

Often cottage cheese from the milk box went missing. Back in 1962 everybody had milk boxes on their porches. There were trucks that delivered fresh milk, cottage cheese, and cream with the skin on top. It was delicious and fattening! In those days we did not worry about fattening foods. Most kids were skinny. We played outside and got dirty, too. Our milkman, Mr. Davenport, brought these wonderful items before dawn. That spring, there were several weeks when my mother asked Mr. Davenport where the cottage cheese was, and he'd reply, "I'm sure I delivered it."

But Mom would say, "No, no, Mr. Davenport. I did not get the cottage cheese. Now don't charge me for it!" She was quite firm.

Poor Mr. Davenport must have thought he was losing his mind, but the mystery was solved when Rinny left the evidence uncovered behind the big pine tree. I don't recall whether he ate the cottage cheese or simply seemed to be motivated by the challenge of stealing it. What I kept wondering was how did he get that milk box open? He was a very smart dog! I don't recall whether Mom ever told Mr. Davenport that Rinny had stolen the goods. I think she just stopped ordering cottage cheese. She would never admit that she was mistaken.

When Chris's pet box turtle disappeared, we figured Rinny was to blame. Fortunately, the turtle managed to dig itself out of the hole. The teeth marks on the shell were what gave Rinny away.

I have a vague memory of Rinny having an affair with Poochie, the dog next door. Or perhaps I think I remember, because Chris said it happened. She was a medium-sized white mutt who was sweet and soft. Since, in those days, few people neutered or spayed their animals (this was not a good thing),

Poochie may have had puppies. Perhaps the incident was covered up. After all, Rinny was practically of royal birth; according to my mother, he had a perfect pedigree with excellent breeding lines. My mom would have been desperate to preserve Rinny's reputation and avoid a scandal.

I always felt that Rinny was my protector. Every night Rinny slept in the living room so he could keep an eye on everyone. In the morning he would make the rounds to each bedroom and thoroughly lick all of our faces to wake us up. He was always on duty.

As a child I was terrified of thunderstorms, and when bad weather rolled in, Rinny would come and cuddle with me. He made me feel safe. It wasn't until years later that I realized he had probably been just as frightened as I was, and we had been protecting each other.

Back then the world was a different place. Maybe it was safer, I'm not sure. If bad things happened, we didn't know about it. Kids walked everywhere, even to school. In fact, our parents generally kicked us out of the house in the morning and expected us to spend the day outside. We may have come home for lunch or eaten at a friend's house—usually peanut butter and jelly on white bread. (In those days kids didn't seem to be allergic to nuts or wheat, or anything, for that matter.)

A bologna sandwich and chocolate milk at Margie's house was my favorite lunch. Margie was my best friend from age five to adulthood. She was a tiny girl with big green eyes and blond hair. We shared a love of animals, especially dogs and horses.

Margie had a collie named Dusty. Back then there was always somebody in the neighborhood who had a collie, because *Lassie* was a very popular television series. After lunch, we would be sent out the door again until dusk, when my mom would ring a big old bell signaling that it was time for dinner, and then home we would go.

Everyone had a dog, but according to my family, Rinny was the best dog in the neighborhood and the world. Life seemed so much simpler, and our parents believed we were safe outdoors to play to our heart's content with a dog by our side. I can still see Mom, tiny and so pretty, but a force to be reckoned with, standing on the top of the back steps, ringing that enormous bell. And I can still hear the loud chimes echoing through the early evening air as we hurried home, our dogs trotting beside us, to see what was for supper.

Rinny passed away peacefully at the age of thirteen but his memory will forever live on in our hearts.

My grandparents with one of their many beloved dogs,
Samos, Greece, 1934

My dad with his favorite dog, Vero, 1935

My most perfect dog, Rin Tin Tin, and me, 1965

Yo, Rinny!

BY CHRIS ILIADES

W HEN I WAS A BOY, dogs could be stars of television shows. There was Lassie, and Roy Rogers's Bullet. But in my eyes, there was only one true star: Rin Tin Tin. *The Adventures of Rin Tin Tin* was a TV series that aired in the 1950s. It was about a boy named Rusty. Boys could be named Rusty in those days.

Rusty lived with a cavalry troop, a German shepherd name Rin Tin Tin, and a kindly lieutenant named Rip Masters. Men could be named Rip in those days. At some point in every episode, Rusty would yell, "Yo, Rinny!" Then Rinny would save someone, or sometimes the whole cavalry troop, including Rip Masters. Anything seemed possible. So when my parents decided it was time to get me a dog, they got me a German shepherd, and of course I named him Rin Tin Tin. *Yo, Rinny!*

To ten-year-old kids like my friends and me, Cedar Grove, New Jersey, was an entire universe. It was so varied in its terrain that we didn't need to use our imaginations to name our special places. There was The Field, The Reservoir, The Pines, The Woods, The Quarry, The Sandpit, The Tracks, The Tunnel, The Trestle, The Brook, and The Pipes. The only evocative name was Devil's Hole, a deep ditch we were sure was haunted. We played, camped, and met in all these special places and explored them endlessly. I was often with Joey, Chucky, Jackie Quinn, and John. There were also a few others who came and went, and there was always Rinny.

The world must have been a better place back then, a safer place for ten-year-old boys. Or perhaps my mom was very naïve or very lenient, or she wanted to get rid of me. As soon as the weather got warm, I was allowed to disappear in the morning with my sleeping bag and mess kit. The gang would meet at one of our secret spots, stay all day, and then cook our own dinner. We'd spread out our sleeping bags and fall asleep under the stars. The only thing I can remember my mom saying was, "If you get into trouble, just send Rinny home." Seriously. Just like Rin Tin Tin on TV, Rinny would run home and get the cavalry. My mom thought this was a perfect contingency plan.

Rinny wore a collar with a dog license, but I never remember him being on a leash. I also don't remember Rinny displaying any less-than-ideal behavior or traits—no barking, no bad breath, and no pooping on anybody's lawn (well, maybe sometimes). Many neighborhood dogs roamed free. There was Boots from down the street and Poochie from next door. Though, of course, the dogs had to have relieved themselves somewhere; perhaps people weren't as freaked out about dog poop back then.

I never remember encountering any rain, mosquitos, or poison ivy during all those nights spent camping in the woods. However, my mom said I had a poison ivy rash so often that I became immune to the plant. I don't react to it now, so that could be true.

In reality, Rinny probably wasn't a perfect dog. I certainly wasn't a perfect kid, but we were perfect for each other. It's been fifty years since Rinny and I roamed the wilds of Cedar Grove. The only people who knew Rinny and are still around are my little sister, Connie, and me. In our family, any time Rinny's name came up, and it often did, the response would always be, "Oh...that Rinny, he was such a good dog." An alternate response was, "That Rinny was the smartest dog ever."

How smart was Rinny? My mom swore he was smarter than most people. Of course, my mom had a low opinion of anyone who was not a blood relative (that included in-laws). Her most frequent descriptive term for any outsiders was "nincompoop."

13

I don't want you to get the wrong idea about my mom. She was different. She put sugar on tomatoes and salt on watermelon. But she was a great mom. The best.

At a quarter to three on school days, my mom would send Rinny to pick us up. To reach school from our house, he had to cut through our backyard and the Canarises' backyard, go down Monroe Street, cut through the Pappases' backyard (there were many Greeks in our neighborhood), and cut through the upper and lower athletic fields. This would bring him to the back door of Ridge Road School.

At five minutes before three, just before the bell rang, I could look out the window next to my desk and see Rinny outside waiting for me. He was even more reliable than the bell. When Mrs. Parker saw Rinny out there, she would get us ready for dismissal. Consequently, all the kids started to look for Rinny at the end of the school day.

One time Rinny saved me from monsters. My friend Chucky lived up the hill from me on Lakewood Avenue. We brought out the worst in each other, and we liked it. For instance, we were both obsessed with monsters. We drew monster pictures, and collected monster magazines and comic books. Our favorite movie was a futuristic, science fiction monster classic called *Frankenstein 1971*. I'm not certain if that was the real title, but 1971 sure seemed very far into the future indeed. It was very scary.

Chucky's and my adventure took place at The Field. Chucky

and I had almost blown up The Field the year before. Chucky's father worked at a plant that made Formica, so his basement was filled with dangerous chemicals. The message to keep toxic substances away from kids was not out back then. So we poured every chemical we could find into a bucket, made a fuse, and buried the bucket in the middle of The Field. We then lit the fuse and hid it among the pine trees. The resulting explosion created a miniature mushroom cloud. Luckily, by the time the Cedar Grove Fire Department arrived, there was nothing left of the bucket that could be traced back to Chucky and me. For the rest of my life in Cedar Grove, there was always a big bare spot in the middle of The Field.

Now back to Rinny and the monsters. There was an abandoned building on the edge of The Field (which was next to The Reservoir.) It was probably a small office that a reservoir official had used long before. It was always just called "The Office." It was always padlocked and deserted. One summer morning when we met at The Pipes to begin our day, Chucky showed up with a big hammer.

"We need to get into The Office. There may be monsters hidden there. Why else would they need to keep it locked up?" asked Chucky.

It was hard to argue with that kind of logic. The padlock was probably thirty years old and it popped off with the first blow. Rinny sat outside and watched us. Being a smart dog, he didn't follow us into The Office. I'm sure that by age ten, I didn't really believe in monsters, but I believed in believing in monsters. I can't speak for Chucky, but obviously Rinny wasn't taking any chances.

The Office had a creaky floor and a coal stove, and was filled with a powerful smell of mold. It contained one door, which we guessed led to a small, attached shed. If there were monsters, they would be behind that door. We pushed it open and found ourselves walking into a low, dark room.

The next thing I remember is falling. My chin and chest scraped the stone wall on the way down. When my mind cleared, it registered very dark, cold, and quiet stillness. Monsters became a real possibility. There was no sound from above.

Chucky was gone. This was not surprising; Chucky could vanish instantly. It usually happened on the way to school.

Then I heard the sweet sound of Rinny barking outside The Office door. I might have yelled, "Yo, Rinny!" I must have closed my eyes and gone into monster shock.

The next thing I knew my mom was calling my name and shining a flashlight down onto my head. What had seemed to be a cavernous tomb was not very impressive once my mom shined the light all around me. It was just a small coal cellar. There were no monsters.

Rinny was still barking and I remember my mother laughing, probably in relief. There were some metal rungs built into the wall opposite from where I had landed. It was a quick climb back to safety, sunlight, and the real world. The sun was warm, The Field was green, and The Reservoir sparkled as if scattered with diamonds. Rinny jumped up and slobbered me with wet kisses.

We went home and mom sent me to the tub. At least I had come away with some impressive scrapes on my chest and chin. I'm sure that when I fell, Chucky ran back to his house and told his mom what had happened, because his mom called my mom. But over the years, in remembering this story, it became only Rinny who had saved me. The coal cellar would become deeper and darker. The whole part about breaking into The Office became Chucky's fault. My mom was good like that. (Well, it *was* his idea.)

Over a lifetime, our memories become our stories, and then they become part of who we are. Part of me will always be with Rinny in my childhood home, even though there will never be another dog like Rinny. And there will never be another place like Cedar Grove in 1959, a time when dogs could be TV stars, boys could be named Rusty or Chucky, and a kid like me could be saved by yelling, "Yo, Rinny!" Anyway, that's my story and I'm sticking to it.

My brother, Chris, the all-American boy, Cape Cod, 1958

A Dog Named Piccolo

WHEN I WAS FIVE, I got my first puppy. His name was Piccolo. He was a bad dog. But I loved him.

He bit people, barked constantly, and enjoyed peeing on clean laundry, furniture, and, if he really liked you, your pant leg.

He was a Chihuahua, we think. His pedigree was questionable.

One of my fondest and most vivid childhood memories is of the time when Piccolo was almost arrested. I was seven years old. The two police officers stood at the front door, looking quite stern. I hid behind my father, holding the little culprit.

"What can I do for you, Officers?" my father asked in a casual, somewhat bored tone. My dad was a town doctor of sorts; everyone knew him. He probably took the tonsils out of every kid in the neighborhood, including all of the police officers' children. Dad never got a speeding ticket, which was amazing because he was a terrible driver.

"Hi, Doc. Hate to bother you..." the older officer began to say.

The younger policeman interrupted. "There's been a complaint from your neighbor about a vicious, destructive dog." He checked his little notebook. "A Mr. Peterson across the street there," he said, gesturing to the house.

"Yeah." Dad took his glasses off and looked the cop in the eye—that was a serious look. "What exactly happened?" My father knew exactly what had happened, since he had seen the whole event. I think he found it quite funny, and he didn't like old Mr. Peterson anyway. I held my squirming little dog tighter.

"Well," the officer said, looking at his notes again, "he says the dog tried to bite him and was digging up his tulips, peeing on his plants. Also says he had to chase him off with a shovel, and almost had a heart attack."

"What type of dog was it? Sounds dangerous." Dad stifled a snicker.

"He didn't say—says it's your dog, though."

"Yeah, I see. Well, this is our dog." I peeked out from behind my Dad's pant leg. Piccolo tilted his spotted head; he seemed to be grinning at the two policemen.

"You mean that dog…that little thing? I don't believe it." The young policeman looked at Piccolo, who was wagging his tail now, as though proud of himself for getting away with his bad behavior, and the man tried not to laugh. Fortunately he did not attempt to pet Piccolo, because a bite to the hand would have ended the fun times.

The older man shook his head. "Sorry, Doc. Your neighbor must have been mistaken. That dog doesn't look too dangerous to me."

"Well, alright then, you officers have a good day." Dad let the screen door slam behind him. Piccolo jumped out of my arms and ran into the living room to pee on the couch. He lifted his skinny leg with what looked like sheer delight. I tried to catch him, but it was too late.

Dad sighed and mumbled, "Damn dog." I cleaned up the pee as best I could, hoping my mom wouldn't notice. Then Piccolo trotted off, undoubtedly looking for more trouble.

It all began when I went with my mother to the home of a distant cousin, whom I didn't know very well. He was older, in his twenties, and owned a Chihuahua named Bitsy. Bitsy had one puppy. I'm not sure if Bitsy was a real Chihuahua—she was kind of big. My cousin kept her and the puppy in a cage on a shelf. While we were visiting, he handed me the tiny dog and said, "Wouldn't you like a puppy?"

I looked at my mother, expecting a negative response. To my amazement she said, "He is cute—let's take him home!"

I was delighted to have a new puppy, but I was a little concerned. Mind you, we already had a dog: our big, noble, and saintly German shepherd Rin Tin Tin. Didn't my mother realize that Rinny may not like this puppy or might even eat him? Even at the age of five I could envision this possibility. It was not a good idea.

But I wanted the puppy. I thought he was so cute. In truth, he was not cute at all. He was funny looking at best. He had buggy eyes, huge ears, and skinny legs, and his coat was mostly white with some brown spots.

Well, we took the puppy home. My father was a little surprised at the new arrival, but immediately suggested, "Let's name him Piccolo, which means 'small' in Italian." Dad thought that was very clever.

Rinny came over to see the new addition to the family. I was scared to let go of Piccolo. My father said, "Put him down on the floor and see what happens." Before I could say anything, Dad scooped up the pup and placed him in front of Rinny. Piccolo immediately began to bark and growl, standing his ground.

My dad snorted, "That is one dumb dog."

Rinny eyed the small animal and then lifted his leg, peed on Piccolo's head, and trotted away. He clearly wanted no part of little Piccolo. Good dog that he was, he tried to ignore the pup, but Piccolo went after Rinny like gangbusters, chasing him, biting his tail and his leg and making him yelp, and generally torturing our poor "good dog" Rinny.

Piccolo was fast. No one could catch him. All afternoon during that first meeting, Rinny tried to get away, but that little pup could move. Finally Rinny grabbed him by the neck and tossed him across the living room like a softball. This presented only a minor setback for Piccolo, who just returned with a vengeance. I finally tackled the puppy and held him tight. However, as soon as I put him down again, he went back after Rinny for more.

This, we discovered, would not get better with time. There was no Dog Whisperer back then. So Rinny would spend part of the day in the basement while Piccolo ran around the house, and then in turn Piccolo would be barricaded in the guest bathroom and Rinny would take over. It was not an ideal situation. But that was how it went.

Regardless, I loved little Piccolo. He had a lot of personality, but he tolerated my dressing him in doll clothes. (Poor dog.) He looked adorable in one particular frilly blue dress. He was my best playmate and constant companion.

My mother had spent much time training Rinny, making him the "perfect dog," which she gave herself full credit for, but

Piccolo proved to be untrainable, despite her best efforts. I am not sure if she really tried very hard, since Piccolo was such a nasty little thing. He loved me, but no one else. He was happy to bite anyone he did not like, which was everybody.

He did have a fondness for my aunt and uncle. When we would travel, Piccolo would take up residence at Uncle Mike's house in the country. I wonder now whether my parents were hoping Piccolo might have an unfortunate accident involving a hungry coyote, fox, or small bear, or perhaps drown in the nearby lake. However, Piccolo seemed to love Uncle Mike and Aunt Annetta so much that when we returned from our vacations he would have all but forgotten us—even me—and would growl and snap at us when we tried to catch him and take him home.

Piccolo had a passion for running free. He was Houdini reincarnated: he could escape from any confinement. We had a fenced-in yard, but it didn't matter; he always got out. He also frequently managed to run out the door and annoy the neighbors. When I started school, Piccolo was kept in the bathroom for a good part of the day. It was the only place from which he could not escape. Unfortunately he showed Mom what a bad idea this was by eating most of the woodwork.

Still, one day Piccolo escaped the bathroom somehow and my mother could not find him. (Though truthfully, I'm not sure if she tried very hard.) No one knew how he had gotten out. In 1962 kids walked to school, and I was no exception. Apparently

Piccolo had decided to follow me. He was also good at breaking and entering, and somehow he made it into Ridge Road School one day. We were in the middle of our morning reading class when, to my surprise, I saw my little dog dash into my classroom, where he ran happily about, ducking under the desks looking for a good place to pee. How he got there, I have no idea. My teacher, old Mrs. Robinson (bless her soul), thought he was adorable until he growled at her. I finally caught him and she sent me to the office to call Mom and ask her to come and pick him up. Mom was not too happy. Piccolo never went to school again. Mom made sure that bathroom was secured!

As every dog owner knows, bad dogs live forever. When he got older, Piccolo developed heart disease and epilepsy, but that didn't slow him down very much. He could still outrun anybody and bite you if he felt like it. He died peacefully at the age of fourteen, surrounded by family and friends.

I remember Piccolo fondly. He was no Rin Tin Tin; in fact, he had no redeeming qualities whatsoever. But he will always be my very first puppy—and he behaved as sweetly as could be with me. We buried him in the backyard under the big pine tree and marked the spot with a little headstone. Piccolo was full of life and definitely made an impression on everyone with whom he came into contact—maybe not always such a good one, but he will certainly not be forgotten by those he met.

My parents never got another dog.

Our Chihuahua Piccolo, 1966

Not a Dog Story
(The Era of Cats)

WHEN I WAS STILL LIVING AT HOME, after Piccolo had passed away, my family began to collect cats. This had not really been their plan. It was my brother's fault. He started a cat collection in college. Chris seemed to come upon all manner of abandoned cats. I secretly believe he was angry that my parents had not allowed us to get another dog after Piccolo.

I'm not really a cat person. Don't get me wrong—I like cats, but I am allergic to them, so the entire time we owned cats I spent sneezing. My Dad (the doctor) told me to get over it, to stop whining! Allergies got no respect back in the day.

Chris would always start off catless in September,

and then somehow end up with one or two by the end of the school year. The problem would arise at the start of the summer break—what to do about those cats when he had to leave his college apartment in Connecticut to go home? Well, he would just bring the cats with him to New Jersey, of course. I think my mom kept thinking that cat ownership was temporary, that a cat or two or six would find other homes, or eventually go to live with my brother after college. Nope, that did not happen.

The first cat was Barbara (she came with the name), a pretty gray tabby who had been abused and was completely nuts. Chris kept her in his dorm room for a while, but soon enough she ended up at our house. Barbara lived under my bed. She rarely appeared, but I liked the idea of having a pet even though I never saw much of her.

More cats followed. There was "Omar of Oxnard" and "Raoul of Bayonne," named after Johnny Carson's tailors. (*The Tonight Show Starring Johnny Carson* was one of my brother's favorite TV shows.) Omar was all white and Raoul was blue-gray; they were very affectionate cats.

Then came Ty and Cosmos, two brothers who did not like each other. Ty was a huge cat who growled like a dog. He could be nasty. We were all scared of him. Cosmos was smaller and very sweet.

I admit that I contributed one cat to the household. It was a chilly, rainy day and I heard mewing outside. I looked out the window and saw a kitten on our back step. He was wet, dirty, and needed love. I took him inside to show my mother and asked her if we could keep him.

"No, put him back. He's somebody's cat."

"But he's cold!"

Mom gave in, and Sidney, cat number six, found a home with us. He was gray and white and very friendly.

So now we had six cats in our house. They all roamed freely, inside and outdoors. They seemed to like the basement most of all; maybe there were mice down there. We lived in an old house with lots of crawl spaces and hidden cubbyholes. It was a great place to be a cat.

Cosmos went missing one day and for almost a week we could not find him. On a Saturday afternoon I was upstairs in the attic, which was our playroom. I was listening to a Beatles record with my friend Margie. We were in a deep discussion about which boys we would have crushes on for the current school year when we were interrupted by some odd sounds coming from the wall behind us.

Every time a song ended, we heard mewing. This seemed strange, since we believed the cats never went upstairs. Could it be Cosmos? My friend Margie and I looked all around—under the couch, in the closet—but we could not find a cat anywhere.

The mewing continued to grow louder and more desperate, as if to say, "I'm here!" We searched and searched the attic but found no cat. The sound seemed to be coming from inside the wall, which made no sense. However, like the basement, the attic had many little cubbyholes and storage spaces. There was a tiny closet with a dormer window that we had not yet checked. Sure enough, the mewing was loudest in there. Somehow Cosmos had wedged himself between the walls of the closet.

But there was no way to get him out without breaking through the wall. It was time to get Dad. He would not be happy about this. I headed downstairs to the den where he was reading, with Margie trailing behind me.

"Dad, I think I found Cosmos!"

"That's nice." He looked over his newspaper and removed his pipe from his mouth. "So we still have six cats."

"Well, there is a little problem—maybe you could help us?" I gave him a hopeful smile. *"Please."*

Dad put down his pipe and followed me upstairs, grumbling to himself. When he heard the mewing, he reminded me that the wall was very nice cedar wood and we didn't need six cats. He then spent the better part of the day breaking though the closet wall to rescue Cosmos.

Cosmos was grateful to be freed and seemed to be just fine in spite of the ordeal. I was happy we found him that day. We still had six cats and would soon have seven!

Chris attended medical school in Guadalajara, Mexico. In what now seemed like a family tradition, he managed to get one more cat home before my parents said, "Absolutely no more cats!" It was a little kitten that Chris had rescued from an irresponsible pet shop in the city. I think he would have taken all the animals he found there if he could. He had raised the tiny, skinny kitten in his house in Mexico and named him Butcher del Bosque, for no particular reason, except that it sounded Spanish. He called him "Butchy" for short, which sounded very American. When summer came along, Chris brought the little cat home aboard an Air France jet. My parents were less than delighted; the last thing they wanted was yet another cat.

However, Butchy quickly became everyone's favorite cat. He was very small with long, silky gray fur, tiny paws, and big blue eyes. He always looked like a kitten. In addition to being extremely cute, Butchy endeared himself to everyone by acting more like a dog than a cat (clearly we needed another dog, but little Butch was as close as we were going to get.) He loved to sit in our laps and follow us around. He would roll over for even more attention.

My mother swore that he was so smart that he could talk. She would buy him freshly sliced baked ham and show it to him, asking, "What do you like, Butchy?"

And that cat would swish his lovely tail and mew the word "*Ham*," I kid you not!

Even my father loved him. They would sit and watch TV together. Butchy liked to perch on his shoulder, or sometimes on his head. Dad would swear at the TV, especially if he was watching the news or a show about politics, but Butchy never seemed to mind, which is more than I can say for my mother.

My grandmother, who lived with us, was also quite fond of Butchy. She would often tell us how much she loved dogs and not cats, especially when she would find cat litter in the kitchen. But Butchy would make his way onto her lap when Dad wasn't home and she would pet him and smile. "I like dogs better, but this cat is like a dog," my grandmother would say in her endearing Hungarian accent.

She would also say other wise things like, "If you don't know what to do, don't do anything," and "If you are hungry, have a piece of bread." If she was pleased with something, she would remark, "Now you're cooking with gas!" Gram had a saying for just about everything.

Butchy lived a charmed life as the favored cat. The other cats did their own thing, ignoring the dog-cat who they seemed to find strange. Eventually all the older cats passed away, leaving only Butchy to rule the house. And then the unthinkable happened: Butchy went missing. You can imagine how devastated we were. Butch loved his home so much that he hardly ever went outside, so we suspected he may have been stolen. My mom combed the neighborhood. She searched for him for days.

Days turned into weeks, and then months. We had all but given up hope, and then one morning Mom was driving along and spotted Butchy in a neighbor's yard. She could not believe her eyes! She jumped out of the car and grabbed him. It was truly a miracle! Butchy came home and settled in as though he'd never left, acting exactly like our beloved cat in every way. We were delighted.

However, there was something a little odd…

When Mom took the cat to the vet for a checkup, it seemed that Butch, whom we had always thought was a boy, was now a girl. This was very surprising indeed. My mother insisted that Butchy had been a girl all along, and that was that. No one argued with Mom or wanted to admit that she may have stolen someone's cat right out of their yard.

And so "Butchy" (as we continued to call her) enjoyed the rest of her life in our loving home.

In the mid-seventies, during this era of all the cats, I left for college. It was a time when there were no cellphones, computers were the size of refrigerators, and gas cost fifty cents a gallon. I drove an orange GTO handed down from my brother. Who would have thought that car would be a collector's dream forty years later? After college I moved back home for a while and worked as a schoolteacher. By that time Butchy was our only pet. She passed away around the time my brother got married and had his first child, who happened to be extremely allergic to cats. The era of cats had ended. Chris finally got a dog!

Chris and I with Cosmos and his brother, Ty,
Cedar Grove, New Jersey, 1974

Kenya,
the Lion Dog

WHILE CHRIS WAS STILL IN MEDICAL school, he and his wife, Karen, spent one Thanksgiving at the home of some friends. They were a lovely couple named Pat and Kris Kennedy, and they were from Connecticut. Their pride and joy was a large hound dog named Katie. On that sunny Thanksgiving Day, nobody would enjoy the enormous turkey that was to be served, or I should say, no *person* would enjoy it.

According to my brother, the large bird was defrosting unattended in the bathtub and Katie happened to find it. She devoured the entire raw turkey—meat, skin, and bones, and even the wrapping. Afterwards, Katie was one happy dog, and she did

35

not get sick, not even a little. The menu changed to hamburgers with all the fixings, sweet potatoes, cranberry sauce, and green bean casserole. Everyone had a very nice time!

Katie was a ninety-five pound Rhodesian ridgeback. The Kennedys had been breeding dogs for years, and when Pat finished school, they decided to breed Katie. She was a beautiful dog, big for a Rhodesian ridgeback, with excellent lines. Katie had several pups. One of the females was a very big puppy, too big for the Kennedys' breeding program, so they decided to find a nice home for her.

At about that time, Chris and Karen had their second child, and it was time to get a puppy. Pat and Kris were delighted to give them their big, sweet girl to love. Chris and Karen named her Kenya, to honor her African roots. She grew into a very big dog, topping off at about one hundred and twenty pounds. She was quite impressive to behold.

A Rhodesian ridgeback was quite an exotic dog in 1979. The Kennedys were trendsetters, as was Chris. Everywhere they went people would stop and ask about their dogs. Ridgebacks are known for the unusual ridge of fur along their spines. They are usually red in color with a soft hound face and floppy ears. They are loyal, strong-willed, mischievous, and sensitive. Originally from South Africa, this dog was bred to guard and hunt. It was known for its ability to stand up to a lion, so it was also called the African lion dog.

Fortunately, Kenya was a very well-behaved girl. Baby number three came along, and the kids regarded Kenya as a big pillow and also a pony. She was patient and sweet. She may have been able to stand up to a lion, but she was a pushover for the kids.

In 1980 the family lived in a duplex near Newark, New Jersey. It was situated close to the Garden State Parkway, not a great area for a big dog, and not a very good neighborhood either. Kenya was a perfect family dog, but could also terrorize the mailman and anyone else she did not trust. This was not a bad thing, considering the area. Eventually the family moved to a lovely house on Cape Cod, where Kenya had a nice big yard to play in alongside the three children.

Kenya was well behaved in the new house and was also generally regarded as a very nice dog in the neighborhood. She was friendly, except with anyone she deemed to be an intruder. She was never vicious, although some people found her to be scary as hell. For some reason, Kenya did not like Karen's brother and growled at him on occasion. However, I always loved her; we were great friends. I was so happy to have a dog in the family again.

Kenya certainly was not perfect. In fact, she had a secret. She loved to wander outside, and my sister-in-law, having three young children, did not know exactly where the dog was at all times. They lived in a neighborhood near the woods with very little traffic. Karen had always assumed the dog was in the un-fenced yard because she seemed to be there when she was called. But Kenya was actually sneaking around the block, stealing a meal or two from unattended picnic tables. I was visiting for the weekend when Kenya was caught red-handed one Sunday morning.

I was outside playing with two of the children—Nick, who was then six, and Tina, who was four. The baby, Corinne (or Cory, as they called her), was napping. It was a gorgeous fall day. I did not notice Kenya leave the yard. She simply vanished.

Later we were able to figure out what probably had happened. Kenya had followed her nose to a nice Sunday brunch. She must have smelled bacon. Her nose had led her to the back-yard of some neighbors. She had likely kept her distance at first and watched them lay out a wonderful feast on their picnic table: eggs, bacon, and buttered toast. The table was set with pretty paper napkins and flowers. Kenya must have waited until the time was right, when the mistress of the house went inside to fetch the pot of hot coffee and the food was unguarded. (Kenya certainly upheld the Rhodesian ridgeback reputation for being mischievous and intelligent on that day.)

She quickly ate everything, including a couple of napkins. But her distinctive ridge of fur was noted as she made her es-cape. The neighbor immediately called my sister-in-law. I watched Karen's face as her smile was replaced by a look of horror. But she did not miss a beat! Right in that moment Kenya arrived with her tail wagging.

"I'm sorry, Mrs. Murphy, Kenya is right here. It must have been another dog." Then, after a moment, she said, "Well, if that's how you feel, I'd be happy to pay for everything..."

There seemed to be silence on the other line. Karen hung up and confessed to me that she believed Kenya was guilty. The dog had egg on her muzzle, so to speak. Apparently, it had not been the first phone call from an unhappy neighbor with missing food.

After that, Chris and Karen decided to fence in their yard and Kenya did not escape too often. She mellowed a little with age. Nick was about twelve when she passed away. She will always be remembered as a gentle giant and a wonderful family dog. Kenya instilled a love of dogs in Chris's children that they would take into adulthood, and her presence signaled the start of a time when dogs would forever be in our lives.

My niece Tina, age four, with Kenya the lion dog, 1984

Our Firstborn Child Had Fur

AFTER PICCOLO, I DIDN'T HAVE another dog of my own until I got married. Before then, I wanted to have a dog but I never lived anywhere that allowed pets. I could not wait to get a puppy. It was a prerequisite of mine that a prospective boyfriend loved dogs. If not, forget it! When I met my husband, it was love at first sight. Thank God, Jim loved dogs as much as I did.

At the time, Jim had a family dog, a Siberian husky named Czar. I mean, what else do you name a Siberian husky? Czar was gorgeous, even when I met him in his old age. He had the bluest eyes I'd ever encountered. In fact, so did everyone else in Jim's family.

Being a husky, Czar enjoyed running. Unfortunately, Czar liked to run away from home just for fun. Jim recalls that often he and his sisters, Kathy and Carolyn, along with their little brother David would anxiously comb the neighborhood, looking for their lost dog. After a while their dad would go looking for him too, in their Grand Safari station wagon. He knew Czar loved to ride in cars. After traveling around, sometimes for several miles, he would eventually spot Czar happily trotting along the sidewalk. As soon as Jim's father stopped, the dog would jump right in the old station wagon for a ride home.

Jim and I were married in 1984. We lived in a tiny apartment in Pittsburgh while Jim attended medical school. The place did not allow dogs. We talked about getting a dog all the time, but we had to wait until we settled in a place where we could have a pet.

In 1986 we moved to New Jersey. The eighties was a time of big hair, Madonna, and shoulder pads, along with some great science fiction movies, such as *The Terminator* and *Dune*. We got our first color TV, which had a screen that measured a full twenty inches. It sat on a shelf made of cinderblocks and plywood. I was fascinated by the new MTV station. We did not have a VCR or a camcorder. There was no Internet; we didn't even have an answering machine. I drove a red Firenza. Jim walked to school.

We had moved into a one-bedroom apartment where dogs were allowed! Life was good. Jim and I discussed at length the breed of dog we wanted. It felt like the most important decision we could possibly make in our lifetimes. After much research we decided on a Pembroke Welsh corgi. The corgi is a small dog with a big dog's attitude, a smart herding dog that can fit in a small apartment. So with our decision made, we went in search of a breeder.

This was no easy task, as corgis were hard to come by in our area. But as luck would have it, my father-in-law worked with a man who happened to breed corgis—not just any run-of-the-mill corgis, but show-quality dogs. I was fascinated. I loved to watch the Westminster dog show on TV every year. Show dogs were special, bred to be the best representation of their breed in both beauty and temperament. So Dad put in a good word for us with Harold Small, the dog breeder, saying we were responsible and would make good puppy parents.

I remember the first conversation I had with Lynne, who was married to Harold. This was back in the day when people used landlines and did not have caller ID.

"Hi! Is this Mrs. Small? I..."

"Who is this?"

"I...um...this is Dr. Newcomb's daughter-in-law, my—"

"Who?"

"Dr. Newcomb, he works with your—"

"Oh, Allan Newcomb. Why are you calling?"

"We are hoping to buy a corgi puppy?"

"Oh really, who is this?"

Oh boy. I again stated my name and gave her as much information as I could manage to blurt out. I started to sweat.

"Well, I have show-quality puppies, you know, very beautiful. I only breed occasionally, and I only sell to show homes as a rule. But Allan is a good friend of Harold's. If you get a puppy from me, you become my family, you know. You say you live close by…that's good. I can send you an application."

Really? I have to apply to get a puppy? "Do you have any puppies available now?" I asked timidly.

"Maybe. We can talk again after I review your application."

"Okay, I—"

She hung up.

After Jim and I meticulously filled out our application, I was granted an interview. So off I went to the lovely corgi-filled home of Harold and Lynne in Far Hills, New Jersey. I don't think I have ever been more nervous. I hoped she would like me. Her house was large, beautiful, and covered in dog hair.

I walked into her kitchen and was greeted by a Bernese mountain dog named Kathy and a dachshund named Rocky, along with several corgis. Lynne invited me to sit down for a moment to chat. She was a tiny, sturdy lady with short dark hair and a bit of a Jersey accent.

"Do you work?" she asked.

I was afraid to give the wrong answer. "Yes, but only four days a week. I'll have plenty of time to spend with a puppy."

Lynne paused for a moment. "Do you want a dog or a bitch?"

"What?"

"That's dog-show talk. Never mind...I pick the puppy for you anyway. I have a boy and two girls right now. I want to see what their conformation is, so I can't let you know which one is available, but I think they will all be show quality. I don't place them until they are at least three months old."

I looked at her blankly.

"Conformation means their show potential." She sighed. "Would you like to see them?"

And with that she disappeared, and the next thing I knew three of the cutest puppies I had ever seen, along with their momma and poppa, were running all around me. It was August, so I had sandals on, and they nibbled my feet like furry piranha fish.

At that moment getting one of those adorable puppies became the most important goal in my life. I had to have one! Lynne said she would be in touch, and I waited nervously as the weeks went by.

In the fall she called to tell me I could have the male, but she would retain stud rights, in case she decided to breed him later on. We went to visit the pup soon after that. Our little boy was adorable.

"Have you ever been to a dog show?" Lynne asked me.

"No, but I watch Westminster on TV."

She just looked at me and snorted. "Well, maybe we can try some handling classes." I had no idea what she was talking about.

So we finally got to take our firstborn son home. We named him Simon.

He was a good puppy, but it was clear from the start that he did not want to be a show dog. Lynne invited me to go to show dog handling classes, but Simon had other ideas. He loved to bark and play with the other dogs, which was not allowed in a show dog class. Lynne kept encouraging me because she thought Simon, like his sisters, might make a good show dog. I tried to train him, but Simon wasn't buying it. I went to some shows with Lynne and Harold, which was fun. I loved to see the beautiful dogs and their skilled handlers. I did not see myself being able to pull it off.

I even went to a corgi club meeting. It was filled with fascinating and strange people speaking their own special language with one another. They said things like, "Did you finish that bitch yet? That's a nice bitch!" and "Does that class bitch have a major?" They used the word bitch in almost every sentence. They were all completely immersed in the show dog world. I felt like an outsider, and I finally gave up when I got pregnant and Simon grew too big for the show ring.

So Simon was just a regular pet and very happy to be just that. He went everywhere with me. He rode shotgun in the front seat of the Firenza, took long walks with me, and kept me company when Jim worked long hours. He was always ready to play fetch outside. He was a social dog who made friends with everyone he met.

Simon's days as an only child came to an end when my daughter was born. I was a little nervous that Simon would be jealous of our new baby. When we brought Margaret home, we gave Simon a new toy, the way some people might for a big brother. He took it and hid under the bed for two days. We were a little concerned. He finally emerged when he was hungry.

However, we needn't have worried; Simon turned out to be a very good big brother. He bonded with Margaret, and especially enjoyed her company when she was old enough to eat baby food. Simon would lick all the leftovers off her and out of the bowl. He got quite fat. When Margaret was in her high chair, she would giggle as she watched Simon hoover up the Cheerios she would throw on the floor.

We moved from our first small apartment into another, and I would walk Simon as much as I could. At the end of the day, we would go pick up Jim from the bus station after work. Margaret, Simon, and I would wait on the platform. Simon attracted a lot of attention. It amazes me that people will more often respond to a dog than a toddler. Margaret was adorable, but most people just talked to the dog!

My son Andrew was born in 1989. We moved to Pennsylvania

when he was two. We lived on a street called Princeton Court, where finally we had a big house and a fenced yard. We lived in a neighborhood full of kids and dogs. By 1993 I had swapped the red Firenza for a silver minivan. Jim bought the kids their first Nintendo game, which, of course, they were too young to play. But Jim had a blast playing it for them. The kids loved to watch and Simon would sit on my feet chewing on a bone.

Simon's herding instinct was strong. He was not happy unless the whole family was in the same room. When we weren't, he would bark and carry on, nipping an ankle or two to make his point.

We fancied Simon to be an excellent watchdog, because he would go nuts when someone came to the door, barking and looking as dangerous as possible, even though he was really very friendly once anyone came in. We felt our home was safe from intruders when we were not home as well. However, this proved to be a delusion when my friend and neighbor Carol told me that she had stopped by on several occasions when we were not home and Simon had not barked at all.

Carol had a key and would stop by when I asked her to let Simon out sometimes. Apparently, when she would arrive, he never came to the door to see who was there. He loved to sleep under our bed upstairs and, in fact, Carol would have to coax him out. He would eventually waddle downstairs and go outside. Then he would come back in, turn away and dismiss her at the bottom of the steps, and go back upstairs to snooze under the bed. Carol reported that, regardless of whether she knocked, rang the bell, or quietly let herself in, Simon never made a peep. Some watchdog!

Simon's best friend in the neighborhood was Carol's miniature poodle, Chip. They would spend time together playing and chewing on their rawhide bones. Every July, Carol would have a birthday party for Chip and invite all the neighbors and their dogs. Simon enjoyed the parties very much. There was a cake for the children and one for the dogs made of dog treats. The adults had a beer or two, and it was great fun.

Simon seldom left our yard; only very occasionally would he get out after someone accidentally left the gate open. But in those instances, I always knew where he was. Carol would call to say that Simon was at her house, and that he and Chip were having a playdate. I would find them happily chewing a couple of bones or playing together.

Simon hated the times we left him to go on vacation. He knew when the suitcases came out that we were most likely leaving for a few days. Before one vacation to Disneyworld, I was happily packing when I noticed Simon was limping. I was very concerned and had no idea what had happened. Simon looked quite pathetic, and I took him in to see the vet right away. She could not find anything wrong, so I took him back home, still limping.

We left for vacation the next day. I felt very guilty. Simon looked at me with sad eyes. Carol was watching him for us. Apparently, as soon as we left, the limp disappeared. It was a miracle!

I dismissed this as a coincidence, until it happened again. A few months later, we pulled out the suitcases and didn't that limp return? Simon used the same trick once more, limping sadly about the house. I ignored him, so after an hour, he gave up and miraculously, there was no more limp! He had made his point.

Simon loved to play. His favorite toy was an old, deflated football. He would bark at people until they threw it for him to retrieve. He would play this game over and over again, barking if the thrower did not do as he pleased. I would buy Simon several beach balls a year, which he would immediately bite at until they deflated. But he always went back to the football.

One day my mother was babysitting at our house. She found the dirty, flattened football in the backyard and threw it away. Simon was beside himself. By the time I realized the mistake, the trash had already been picked up, so I had to make a trip to the sporting goods store to get him another football. He worked on that ball all afternoon to get it just right, all squashed and dirty. And then the barking started; he had some catching up to do. I told my mom to play with him. She never touched his toys again.

Simon would eagerly await his walk before bed, which happened every evening around nine or ten o'clock. This nighttime ritual was Jim's task. Though he doesn't smoke any longer, at that time my husband enjoyed doing so in the evening, and he would sometimes prepare for the walk by carefully clipping the end of a nice Cuban cigar. The sound made Simon come running.

Simon was always prominent in our lives. Jim and Margaret were in a dad-and-daughter club called Indian Princesses when Margaret was about five, along with our neighbor Bryan and his daughter, Kaitlyn. This was a good way to bond with your daughter, Bryan said. One important ritual for the dads was to pick a Native American name for themselves. Jim's was "Walks with Dog." The dads would take the girls camping on weekends. Apparently, while the children played in the woods, the men would drink beer and smoke cigars. I'm not sure who was bonding with whom. Simon did not go with them on these trips, but he was always honored because Jim had the best name in the group.

Simon was a special dog who was full of personality. I loved him dearly. He died of cancer on his tenth birthday. I was devastated; I truly thought I would never recover. I still miss him. He was my doggie soul mate, always there for me, through good times and bad. When Simon was with me, I was never alone; even if Jim worked long shifts or the kids were sick, he was always by my side. I can still feel his soft fur as he sat on my feet when we would watch TV in the evening after the kids went to bed.

From that time on, I always had more than one dog at a time. However, Simon was our firstborn fur child, who lived with us when our human children were babies until they started school. And while many dogs would follow, there would never be another Simon.

My beloved Simon, 1988

Two Greyhounds

THERE ARE TOO MANY depressing stories about greyhounds. Fortunately, awareness has grown over the years regarding the terrible treatment of many retired racing dogs of this breed. Dedicated rescue organizations have successfully found homes for many healthy young dogs who otherwise would have perished. This is a happy story about two special greyhounds.

In 1990, after Kenya, their first dog, passed away, Chris and his family went in search of another dog. By chance they came upon two women who had made it their mission to rescue greyhounds from the local racetrack. The track has long since been closed, but at the time, retired animals as young as three years old were simply euthanized. Appalled by this, these women took all of the abandoned dogs and found homes for them. Through their organization, my brother's family adopted two adult females, aged around three and five years old.

Over the years, people have gradually realized what excellent pets these beautiful animals make. The American Kennel Club describes the greyhound as "swift as a ray of light, graceful as a swallow, and wise as a Solomon." The greyhound can be traced back to ancient Egypt, as early as 2900 BC. It is an elegant breed; these dogs are patient and gentle, and possess soulful eyes that draw people to them.

Chris named the two greyhounds Cleo and Cairo, in keeping with their Egyptian heritage. At that time the family still lived in Cape Cod, but in a larger home near the beach. It was a perfect place for a greyhound. The dogs could run on the beach as they pleased, and greyhounds love to run!

Chris and his wife Karen, along with their children—thirteen-year-old Nick, eleven-year-old Tina, and eight-year-old Cory—enjoyed walking and running with the glorious dogs. Cairo, the older dog, had been quite the champion racer in her prime. She was all gray and had huge thigh muscles and long, strong legs. Cleo, who had not been as successful on the track, was all white and quite attached to Cairo.

Chris and his family recalled that at first the dogs were very quiet and reserved. They would not take a treat from your hand.

They did not bark, even when the doorbell rang. They would walk perfectly on a lead: keeping a steady pace by the walker's side, stopping when he or she stopped, never tugging, and being completely obedient. They were polite, but not anxious for attention. The dogs chose to sleep on the hard floors, not on the couch or beds. They did not know how to go up stairs. They had to be taught. They had lived all of their lives in a kennel.

Gradually, all of this changed. The dogs became accustomed to a loving home. They realized that treats were yummy, soft dog beds were lovely, and the couch was nice, too. Who needed a walk on a leash when you could run free by the ocean? The best part was barking, barking at everything! Getting a belly rub and a scratch on the head was pretty nice, too. They went from being quite thin to looking well fed. It was good to be a pet dog.

While Cleo and Cairo enjoyed the newfound freedoms their family's home allowed, there were a few habits they could not break. For one thing, their need to run in a circle was very strong. They had always raced around a track. They would sprint in giant circles on the beach, chasing each other to their hearts' content! Chris described watching them as "thrilling, as if they were flying."

The other issue was that although greyhounds may love water, they generally cannot swim! However, Cleo and Cairo loved to lie in the shallow bay. On occasion Chris or Nick would find themselves having to rescue the dogs from rising tides.

Another strong instinct for a greyhound is coursing. Originally bred to hunt small game, greyhounds cannot resist the urge to chase anything that moves. If a rabbit came into Cleo's or Cairo's view, it did not have a chance. Woe to the ill-fated bunny who ventured into the yard. It was not a pretty sight. The dogs would catch the critter and toss it into the air, playing with it as though it were a stuffed toy.

This instinct was not necessarily limited to small game. During one walk to the beach with Chris and Karen, Cleo and Cairo encountered a nasty bull terrier who was not on a leash and poised to attack. The greyhounds did not seem fazed; they simply worked together, circling the aggressive dog until he was so dizzy that he gave up.

They were inseparable, but Cairo was the boss. Cleo did not do anything without her roommate. They were some happy pooches. Cleo and Cairo lived to a ripe old age in their happy home. When they finally passed away, they did so within months of each other, Cairo first, and then Cleo. The family remembers their beauty and transformation from kennel dogs to content pets. The children grew up and went off to college, got married, and rescued more dogs, making more pet memories and stories of their own.

But the dogs of their childhood would forever be honored and remembered with sweet fondness. At family gatherings

stories have been passed to the next generation, perhaps sometimes with a little embellishment, but always with a smile.

Nick, Corinne, and Tina with the greyhounds, Cape Cod, 1991

The Real Dogs of Princeton Court

F OR TWO WEEKS OF MY ADULT LIFE, I did not have a dog. They were the worst fourteen days I ever spent. Fortunately, since the summer of 1996, I have always had at least two dogs in my home.

When Simon passed away, I was so sad. The void in our home was incredibly deep. I knew I could never replace him, but I was desperate for another corgi. I loved everything about the breed. I called Lynne, the woman who had given us Simon, but she had no puppies available. I searched and searched for a puppy with no luck. Corgis were still quite hard to come by in our area. And then I happened upon a local breeder, Michele, who asked if I would be interested in adopting an older dog who needed a forever home. She wanted to place one of her retired show dogs.

So we made a date to get together. I was so excited to meet Michele and the corgi, Rae Ann, which I thought was an odd name for a dog, or even a person, for that matter. When the agreed-upon date arrived, I set out with my children, Margaret, who was ten, and Andrew, who was eight, to a small town near Reading, Pennsylvania.

We came to a little house in the country and Michele, along with several corgis, greeted us at the door. Rae Ann was a beautiful dog, a perfect representation of her breed, and very friendly. Michele proudly told us that she came with an impressive pedigree. She had been a successful show dog and had also been a mom, twice! Rae Ann had delivered two litters of pups, a total of eighteen puppies. Many of her offspring had become champions. One of them was still living with Michele and we got to meet her. The pup's name was Hannah and she was just starting her show career.

"Rae is a chow hound, but Hannah won't eat anything! She only seems to like tuna fish," Michele said. She got some small dog treats and tossed one toward the dogs. Rae Ann made an impressive catch in midair. Hannah was not the least bit interested.

"I really don't want to give her up, but I have too many dogs. She should go to a loving home," Michele added, a little sadly.

"I promise she will be well loved," I replied.

(I just recently saw Michele at a dog show. Even though it has been eighteen years since she gave us that wonderful corgi, she seemed to recall Rae Ann vividly and with tremendous fondness.)

And so we adopted Rae Ann. She was four years old when she came to live with us. We had her spayed and she became our beloved pet. Of course, she could not replace Simon, but she made us all so happy. Just putting my face in her soft fur was incredibly comforting.

Rae adjusted quickly to life with us. She was well trained and very pleasant, and behaved perfectly in our home. But she had spent her entire life in a kennel, so it was a big change for her to have the run of the house. Though we had no need to crate her, she was used to sleeping in a one. We allowed her up on the bed with us at night, but she kept jumping off in search of her crate, so we hauled it upstairs and propped the door open. She was delighted to snuggle in there when she was tired. Rae enjoyed dozing on her back in the crate, which looked odd; she would sleep with her furry behind pointed out and her short legs up in the air.

We got Rae Ann a ball to chase, but she was not interested. Instead she preferred to chase rabbits and squirrels that appeared in our yard. And she would quickly dispatch one if she caught it.

We learned that Rae was afraid of thunderstorms, which is not unusual for a dog. During a bad storm, she would try to go into the basement, where she would pee on the floor. She was also afraid of flash photography. Whenever she saw a camera, she would run and hide. The flash must have made her think of lightning. It was difficult to take a picture of her inside the house.

We bought her many new toys, but she only cared for one: a big stuffed hamburger. She liked to toss it in the air, just for a minute or two, and then she was done, ready for a snack and a nap.

My most poignant memory with Rae is from September 11, 2001. I remember the day vividly. I was at home in Allentown, Pennsylvania, a little less than two hours from New York City. We traveled into New York often, and had just recently eaten at the restaurant Windows on the World. The view had been spectacular.

The news of the World Trade Center attack was so shocking that it was hard to comprehend. I stepped outside just to breathe, and sat down on the steps in the backyard. Rae came over to sit next to me. It was a perfectly beautiful day. The September air was crisp, and the sky was cloudless and very blue. And the world would never be the same.

There was complete silence outside—everything had stopped. There was no traffic, no planes, not a sound. I sat with my dog, petting her thick red coat, and I cried. We shared a moment I will never forget.

Not long after Rae Ann came to live with us I went to a pet shop. Normally I would not go to a pet store that sold puppies. (There were still a few of these stores left in our area at that time; fortunately, they have since closed.) But we owned two small lizards that ate crickets, and I could only find crickets at this particular pet store. Walking into the shop that day changed our lives. I didn't even want to look at the pups, but one caught my eye. I had to take him home with me. He was a tiny, two-pound tan-and-black Pomeranian. I just could not leave him there.

When Jim came home that day, he was a little surprised at the appearance of this new pup. I remember him saying, "What the hell is that?" and "It's too small, take it back."

Well, Charlie, as we named him, came with a "no return" policy. If he hadn't, we might have returned him. He was as nasty as he was cute, and he was adorable. He was a little tyrant who liked to bite people.

Rae Ann and Charlie got along okay, but she wasn't crazy about him. What was I going to do?

We did the best we could to socialize Charlie and bring his behavior in line. At great expense, I even hired a professional trainer—two in fact. They loved him; he did not even attempt to bite them. With a great deal of patience and after consistent positive training, Charlie eventually turned into a pretty stable guy. He grew into a stunning dog, topping off at about fourteen pounds. This is rather large for a Pomeranian; dogs of this breed are only supposed to weigh three to seven pounds. He was not fat, just big! His pedigree was questionable.

We were grateful that Charlie turned into such a delightful little pet. But he had some strange habits. He barked at imaginary friends. He loved to play all the time, especially chasing bugs. We realized that it didn't matter whether there was even a real bug. All you had to say was "Charlie, where's the bug?" and he would go nuts, spinning and barking. It was quite funny to watch, and we would prompt him constantly. He never got tired of the game.

Rae and Charlie eventually became good friends. We took walks together. And I realized something: I really liked having two dogs and they liked having each other. I didn't feel bad leaving them; they were quite content with each other's company.

So from that time on, we had more than one dog in our lives. More dogs meant more fun! The neighbors on Princeton Court caught onto this mantra and our local dog community grew. Carol and her family added a friend for Chip into their household, a miniature schnauzer whom she named Dale, so now they had Chip and Dale. My neighbors Becky and Tom got two dogs for their children: a basenji and a pug.

Becky first chose the basenji, Lucy, because the breed is called "the barkless dog"; the shape of their larynx prevents them from barking. Becky describes Lucy as having been smart and independent. She loved to cuddle and was known as a heat-seeking missile in their house. Becky often said that Lucy's serious expression (she usually had a furrowed brow) made them smile.

Then Becky and Tom wanted a companion for Lucy, so Becky chose a pug, only because he was so cute. She named him Ricky. Becky has described Ricky as the "eternal optimist," always happy and just looking for a ball to chase.

My other neighbors Robin and Mark had two little schnauzers in their family, Misty and Mogul. Mark once told me about their breakfast routine. He would make buttered toast for the dogs and then for himself. When he and Robin traveled, he insisted that the dog sitter also carry on this morning ritual.

More neighbors added dogs to their families, and Princeton Court became the street of many dogs. We all watched our children and dogs grow up together. Our kids went off to college, and we all gained some weight and then lost some. Cell phones and email accounts became the only way to communicate. Everyone went on Facebook, even some of the dogs—Ricky had his own Facebook page!

Our dogs were always included in our neighborhood parties. We discussed their many trips to the vet, what we fed them, and their funny traits. Ricky was by far the silliest dog. Lucy was very serious. Charlie was a little nuts—I can still picture him playing with his invisible bug. Rae Ann, in my opinion, was the prettiest and most regal. The dogs of Princeton Court were very special indeed.

All of our children grew into wonderful adults and flourished, but our dogs grew old. The dogs we had watched our children grow up with passed away. The neighborhood is now full of empty nesters, and some of us have gotten more pets. Carol brought home two rescue dogs, Tilly and Bennie. Becky moved away and then moved back again. Their dog Lucy recently passed away at the age of seventeen. New neighbors came with more dogs. When we get together with old friends, we always talk about our family dogs and share wonderful memories, lots of tears, and great love.

Our daughter, Margaret, age ten, with our Corgi Rae Ann, 1998

Margaret and our son, Andrew, at our Pomeranian Charlie's
second birthday party, 2000

Only the Good Die Young

SHE CAME WITH THE NAME GARCIA, and it stuck. Although I think my brother, Chris, had many names for her...none of them flattering. I don't remember that Garcia was such a bad dog; she always seemed to behave when I was visiting. I often sat with her on my brother's couch and petted her shiny coat. Maybe she was a good actor.

What I do know is that Garcia was one lucky dog. She was rescued twice, was well loved, and lived a very, very long life. She looked like a small black Labrador retriever. But she was a mix of many breeds, including pit bull and chow chow.

When my niece Tina was about sixteen, she followed in the family tradition of collecting unwanted animals and took in Garcia, a puppy nobody wanted. Garcia adored Tina, and Tina adored her. They were a perfect match. When Tina went to college, Garcia was left in Tina's parents' house in Cape Cod. It was only temporary—eventually Tina and her sister, Cory, took Garcia back to school with them, which was good because their parents did not really want a dog at that time in their lives. And unfortunately, Garcia simply did not like them. In fact, she would not come near them and was only happy with the children. She was not aggressive with them, just uninterested.

But Garcia was frighteningly dog-aggressive. She spent many a lovely summer running on the beach, digging enormous holes, and terrifying other dogs in the neighborhood. She was also strong and fast. She scared the hell out of a lot of people as well. When she was angry, she looked like a hound from Hell, with a flaring nose, red eyes, and lots of sharp teeth. The children had a way of calming her and kept her under control.

After college, Tina and her boyfriend Mike got married, and Garcia went to live with her beloved master. Tina and Mike loved Garcia very much and they somehow managed to keep her out of trouble, even though she still did not like strange dogs. Luckily she got along very well with the other dogs in the family. She was pampered and adored well into her old age.

When Garcia was about fifteen, Tina and Mike thought she was at death's door. Her kidneys started to fail. Heartbroken, they took her to the vet, who said he could give her some comfort by flushing the kidneys a bit, but that she probably would not live much longer. They said, "Do it!"

When they got home, Garcia perked up remarkably—so much so that she went after the dog next door, growling and snarling like her old self. It was a miracle! Garcia went on to live for two more years and died at the age of seventeen-and-a-half. As they say: Only the good die young!

Tina described Garcia as "a free spirit and fiercely loyal to those she loved....She lived life to the fullest and was always up for an adventure. Garcia loved a long walk on the beach, but at the end of the day, she mostly loved to snuggle on the couch." Tina told me, "I miss her every day."

In spite of these testimonials, and my failure to remember Garcia as being a bad dog, anecdotal evidence suggests that she was very bad indeed. The legend of Garcia is epic and the stories are frightening, especially the one where my brother was nearly arrested and the dog was almost shot by an angry neighbor. But I will let Chris tell that one...

Tina saying good-bye to Garcia before going off to college, Cape Cod, 2002

Garcia

BY CHRIS ILIADES

G ARCIA ARRIVED IN OUR LIVES when the kids were all still living at home. Tina and Nick were in high school and Cory was in eighth grade. Garcia came to us by way of Tina's first boyfriend, who saved the puppy from a house of irresponsible, or at least disreputable, friends of an older brother. I never really understood the whole story. It was one of those things I didn't pay much attention to until it was too late.

As a puppy, Garcia looked like a small, shiny black missile. She had tiny paws, a wide body, short legs, a large head, and a huge attitude. Her origins were obscure, but her head and brain appeared to be those of a pit bull. She seemed to instinctively know that the kids were her allies and my wife and I were her competition.

The first sign that something was horribly wrong with Garcia came when my wife Karen and I decided to take her for a walk at the beach. She was a cute pup and liked the water right away. It seemed like a harmless idea to let her off the leash so she could play in the shallow water.

Bad idea. The moment we released her, Garcia transformed into a trouble-seeking missile. She bolted down the beach until she found a grandmother carrying a small child. She then proceeded to run around Grammy while barking incessantly. It was not a cute puppy bark. It was the sound of the Devil voice coming out of a possessed child in an exorcism movie. Grammy held the baby, who was screeching, up high, and tried to escape down the beach, with my wife and me in pursuit. Soon we were running widening circles around Grammy, trying to catch Garcia while apologizing profusely, and feeling like idiots.

After Garcia tired of tormenting Grammy, she took off to torture a young family enjoying a quiet, sunny morning on a beach blanket. She began circling and barking at a frantic rate. It brought to mind the poem by Yeats titled "The Second Coming":

Turning and turning in the widening gyre…
Things fall apart; the centre cannot hold;

Mere anarchy is loosed upon the world...
The ceremony of innocence is drowned...

Oh, how I would have drowned Garcia at that moment if only I could have caught her! How much aggravation and embarrassment I could have saved myself....What passionate intensity she had.

I am ashamed to say that my wife and I eventually gave up. We left Garcia at the beach, pretended she was not our dog, ran home, and sent the kids back to get her. Luckily, Garcia was never vicious, she was just demented.

As you read this, and as I write this, you may be asking yourself, as I am, why we didn't get rid of that dog right then and there. It may be that we felt she needed to be saved. She had started life on the wrong foot. The kids all seemed to love her. When we told them we had left Garcia at the beach, they looked at us as though we were child abusers. In a way, we were, but we were the ones who felt abused. As soon as the kids got to the beach, Garcia ran up and jumped into my youngest daughter's arms. Round one went to the dog.

Garcia quickly turned our children against us. She and the three kids lived upstairs, where the kids' rooms and television were. Up in their little world, it was all love and cuddles, with Garcia nuzzling in on the couch and sharing their beds. We would imagine them up there plotting against us as we heard their muffled laughter and Garcia's frantic tail beating against the floor.

Downstairs my wife and I were isolated and ignored. Garcia only came down to eat or demand to be taken out to pee or poop. It seemed the upstairs cabal had decided these duties would be delegated to us.

Since the kids and my wife went off to school and work before I did, it was my duty to crate the animal before I left the house. This would involve a ten- to fifteen-minute brawl during which I would throw things and back the dog into a corner, where I could jump on her, and then wrestle her into the crate. Afterwards, the house would look like a crime scene.

I gave up on the crate after the first week, but Garcia never forgave me. (She would not warm up to me until about age twelve.) By the time she was one year old, Garcia still had small feet and short legs, but she was deep-chested and powerful. She had small ears, a big broad head, and that thin, frantic tail.

Our relationship did have some lighter moments. Garcia loved the beach, and despite her small paws, she was an enthusiastic and powerful swimmer. Taking Garcia anywhere on a leash was a shoulder-jolting, foot-sliding, exhausting, and embarrassing mess. She would go around trees and telephone poles just to get stuck on the other side. It was not that she was too dumb to double back; she was actually quite smart. She just wanted to make me give in and come around to her side of every obstacle.

My solution for the beach was to tie a thirty-foot rope on her collar. Once I had brought her to a deserted part of the beach, I would let her go free. The drag of the line allowed me to get into a range where I could catch up to her. Sometimes I could let her go free for a long while. She would chase seagulls, crash into the surf, and launch herself from the tops of sand dunes. I have never seen a dog so completely taken with being a dog. This was a side of Garcia I came to respect. She embraced her freedom and who she was with total commitment. On the best days, with the sunlight scattered over Vineyard Sound like a blanket of diamonds, and the stones rolling in the surf, we enjoyed a kind of bond, or at least an uneasy truce.

As I have grown older, I have become more liberal in my views. This includes a strong belief in gun control. I often say that in my sixty-four years, there has never been an occasion when I wished I owned a gun.

But that is not quite true. There was one time. By the time Garcia was two years old our two eldest children had left for college. It's a good thing I didn't own a gun, because I would have shot the kids' dog and they never would have forgiven me.

Garcia must have been planning her great escape for a while, because her timing was perfect. I was on my way to work in the morning. Everyone else had left. I opened the door, and as I was gathering my keys and picking up my briefcase, she charged past me and blew right through the screen. Unfortunately, Mr. Collins, the district attorney for Cape Cod and the Islands, was leaving his house at the exact same time. I could hear the classic Garcia bark coming from down the street. I ran out to the end of the driveway to find Garcia chasing the man around his car as he tried to ward her off with his briefcase.

Moments later, our meanest neighbor, who lived at the end of our street, made the mistake of going out to get his newspaper. This was good for Mr. Collins but bad for him. When she tired of torturing our most distinguished neighbor, Garcia bolted down the street and chased the meanie back into the house. She then set up shop on his front porch and began to bark happily and incessantly.

It did not take long for the dog officer to arrive. I was chasing Garcia around the mean neighbor's house as he yelled at me from his window, threatening to shoot the dog, who was making his sickly wife's condition worse.

"Do it," I said. "Shoot the dog. I can't stop her."

Officer June was meant to be a dog officer. She wore her pale green uniform smartly and had lots of badges and gadgets, but she was about to have the worst day of her career. After calmly explaining to my mean neighbor that he could not shoot the dog, she assured him and me that she would shortly have everything under control.

Five hours later, Officer June was looking less smart. Her red hair had become a wild tangle around her flushed, freckled face. Perspiration dripped from her nose and her pale green uniform was dark with sweat and dirt.

To her credit, she did have lots of tricks and she was almost as relentless as Garcia. She had tried dog whistles and long sticks with retracting loops—she even tried to lasso the dog like a cowboy. At one point she and I were both hiding with a net to throw over Garcia if the dog took the bait of a bowl of fresh honey ham. Garcia must have been hungry, and she loved ham, but she was way too smart to fall for such a stupid human trick.

After a break for lunch, we started back in. Garcia would sit a safe distance away at the edge of the woods. She was having such a good time. At about three o'clock in the afternoon, my daughter Cory got home from school. She saw the dog officer's truck and June and me sitting on the deck having coffee. We had given up by then. I was trying to reassure June that her career choice was still valid.

"What's going on, Dad?" asked Cory.

"Garcia has been out all day. Everyone in the neighborhood is in lockdown. Officer June has been doing her best, but Garcia has beaten her. Decisively," I said.

Cory turned on her heel and yelled, "Garcia, you get over here right now!"

Garcia trotted across the yard from the edge of the woods and happily followed Cory into the house.

About one year later, a local police officer who had been my patient as a boy knocked on my door. I recognized him right away. His mother had dragged him in for every cold and sniffle.

"Hi, Kevin. What can I do for you?" I asked.

"Doc, I thought I better come over and tell you there is an outstanding arrest warrant out for you," said Kevin. "You never paid a citation from the dog officer that was issued last year."

I immediately paid the citation. Officer June had given up being a dog officer. Years later I found out she had gotten her EMT certification. Getting humans into an ambulance was probably a lot easier for her than wrangling hounds from Hell.

By the time Garcia was six years old, we had moved to a house on the outskirts of Barnstable Harbor. It was just my wife, the dog, and me living together by then. I had made a fenced-in side yard for Garcia, and life had settled down for all of us.

One morning I let Garcia out the side door as usual, but when I went to let her in later on, the yard was empty. All that was left was a pile of fresh dirt and a Garcia-sized tunnel under the fence. Garcia was gone.

I drove around the neighborhood, but there was no sign of

her. That night, at about midnight, I woke up to hear Garcia barking outside on our neighbor Uda's back porch. Uda was a lovely German woman who lived alone. She had often tried to befriend Garcia, but Garcia would just bark relentlessly at her. If Uda was outside working in her garden, I would have to bring Garcia into the house.

I got up and chased Garcia off Uda's porch. Then my wife and I drove around in the car with the back door open. Garcia loved riding in the car, so sometimes this trick would work. But Garcia had gone underground again.

She was gone all the next day. I secretly began to hope we had seen the last of her, but deep inside I knew she would be back.

On the second night, which was windy, we thought we heard her barking, but it was a far-off sound drowned out by the gusts. From our upstairs window, we could see the tidal flats and the lighthouse that marked the entrance to the harbor. At low tide the flats would extend for hundreds of yards out to the channel. I got out of bed and went to the upstairs window, then called my wife to come and look. The moon was full. The tide was all the way out. Moonlight reflected off the sand. Beyond the tidal flats, the dark waters of the harbor ebbed out to the sea. The only other movement was a small black speck of a dog charging across the flats at full speed, barking wildly at the moon and the tide.

The next day Garcia came back, with slobber covering her head and her tongue hanging out. She slept for two days.

Soon after Garcia's episode of moonlight madness, she went to live with my daughters in Boston. When my daughter Tina got married, she went to live with Tina and her husband Mike. Garcia was out of our life, except for visits home with the kids. Mike and Tina loved her deeply and treated her like a queen. She was great with our first grandchild, and she even seemed to warm up to me during her visits.

By age twelve she was still healthy, but her great escape days were long gone. She would still get her back up and bark at any perceived threat, but she couldn't see or hear very well, so the threats were mainly in her mind. Perhaps she was seeing Uda or Mr. Collins in the trees and bushes of her backyard.

Mike and Tina cared for her as though she was their baby until they had their first real baby. After that Garcia gradually began to fail, and was put to sleep at age seventeen. The kids were all devastated. The dog had been deeply loved.

It would be nice to say that I, too, came to love Garcia, but that would be untrue. Let's just say that I came to respect her as a force of nature. No dog ever had a longer or better life than Garcia. Over the years I have come to believe that reincarnation makes the most sense—it is quite possible that Garcia was a saint or a Buddha in a former life who decided to come back and start over for the fun of it. Just to enjoy the heck out of being a dog. How else can you explain all that great karma for such a bad dog?

Corinne and Garcia, 1999

The Wizard
of Food

ALTHOUGH PUERTO RICO is a paradise for tourists, it is also known for its poor treatment of stray dogs. Fortunately, conditions for the animals there have been improving slowly in the past few years. Animal rescue groups have raised awareness of the problem and brought many puppies from the island to the U.S. for adoption.

Ten years ago a little black shepherd-like puppy began his life in San Juan, but made it to the U.S. border. When Nick (my nephew and Chris's son) graduated from college, he learned about the dogs of Puerto Rico, and wanted to adopt a puppy. Nick found the pup at a local shelter. He said that "he looked so scared, I just had to take him home." He named the dog Niko.

Nick describes Niko as "way too smart to be well-behaved." He loves the outdoors and so does Nick. When he goes mountain biking, Niko "runs circles around him." Nick says, "He always makes me smile. His funny little hook tail wiggles his whole body."

From the start Niko was clearly resourceful. He can steal food from anywhere. Any food left on a counter will be gone in a flash. He was born on the street and his instinct to survive is strong. Even though he is very well-fed in Nick's home, Niko just cannot help himself. Everyone in the family has learned not to leave food out if Niko is around. Chris calls him "the Wizard of Food." Niko can open garbage cans, refrigerators, and any door at all with ease. He is almost as adept in using his paws as humans are with their hands. He can also consume anything, including long-dead animals he finds in the woods, without getting even the least bit sick.

Niko is incredibly clever and good at covering his tracks. On one occasion Chris had picked up some delicious take-out fried chicken for the family dinner. He had placed the box of chicken on the counter far out of Niko's reach—or so he thought. When his wife Karen came home she asked, "Who ate all the chicken?" Chris came into the kitchen to find the box exactly where he'd left it, as if undisturbed, but completely empty. He insisted, "We haven't touched it!"

All eyes turned to Niko. Now that was damn clever. Niko certainly is a professional food stealer, a true wizard of food.

Garcia and Niko became good friends. Garcia knew Niko would win any fight she might consider, so from the very beginning, they enjoyed each other's company. Niko taught Garcia the best ways to steal yummy people food.

At one family gathering, someone left cupcakes on the kitchen counter. As soon as the humans left the room, Niko and Garcia somehow managed to get the cupcakes off the counter and eat every one. What was really amazing was that they also hid the wrappers on the floor under the cabinets, so the evidence was gone! When Nick returned, he found no trace of the cupcakes. However, Garcia's face was covered in vanilla frosting. Garcia was not as slick as Niko!

I personally remember being a victim of a cheese drive-by. I was visiting Chris, and so were Niko and Nick. I had brought a nice cheese plate to share with the family. I left the plate on the kitchen counter and stepped outside for just a moment, and when I came back in, the plate was exactly where I'd left it, although it was cleaned off as if it had been washed. There had been quite a lot of cheese. I looked in the fridge, assuming someone had put the cheese away. But then I realized that nobody had been inside the house. I saw Niko in the dining room, looking at me and wagging his tail, as if to say, "Boy, are you clueless!"

I was amazed. That dog truly is a magician.

Other than being a food-stealing addict, Niko is a good dog. He and Nick are the best of friends. Nick recently married a lovely girl named Jennifer, and the three of them are one happy family. Jenn loves Niko as much as Nick does and shared one of her favorite stories about him which follows....

Niko

BY JENN ILIADES

WHEN I MET NICK AND NIKO in 2008, I managed to win both of their hearts. We were married in 2012. My parents, especially my dad, became extremely fond of Niko, and now often they take care of him when we travel. One of the funniest stories that I've heard about Niko is from the first time my parents watched him overnight for us while Nick and I were away for the weekend.

Niko has these big, sad-looking eyes, which he always uses to his advantage. They basically make you want to do anything possible to make him happy! I'm pretty sure this is done on purpose. When it was time for bed, my dad kept looking at the dog and his big, sad eyes and thought that he was upset and missing us. Dad brought his blanket and pillow downstairs onto the living room floor so he could keep the dog company while he slept that night. He fell asleep with Niko cuddling next to him and finally settled down.

Once the sun rose, my dad began to wake up, sore and achy from sleeping on the floor. He looked around and saw that Niko was no longer next to him. Instead the dog was looking down at my dad from his favorite recliner, as though he were thinking he was an idiot for sleeping on the hard floor! My dad then decided to reward his naughty behavior by grilling up a steak and frying an egg. Not for himself, but for Niko's breakfast!

Needless to say, my parents' house is one of Niko's favorite places to go, and he is the most spoiled grand-dog ever! Niko certainly is one smart and lucky dog.

Niko, dreaming of turkey dinner, Thanksgiving, 2005

Harper

BY CORINNE ILIADES SHEH

DOGS HAVE BEEN A PART OF MY LIFE since I was born; I do not believe I have ever been without one. My family just seemed to end up with one right after another, and sometimes a few at once. I loved them all and considered them to be part of my family, but Harper, my current dog, is my first dog as a grown-up with my own little family.

In 2009 my husband, Lawrence, and I had just gotten engaged. Lawrence wasn't so sure about dogs, but he knew that one of the few ways to my heart would include a pup, so he spent weeks online doing research about possible breeds. When I told him I felt we should just go to a shelter and pick one out, he began researching shelters and available litters. He loves to research everything.

I, on the other hand, can be rather impulsive. I don't think my family researched any of our dogs. Each one of them just seemed to fall into our laps. Some were purebred and some were mutts. Some were crowd-pleasing and some only an owner could love. But we loved them all, so I knew Lawrence and I would end up with the right dog simply because once a dog has imprinted on you with those soulful eyes, well, that's it. You're hooked.

The day finally came when Lawrence excitedly explained to me that he had found a litter of hound mixed puppies that had been born in a shelter. The mother had come in as a stray and sadly died shortly after giving birth to eight pups. He theorized that since they had all been bottle-fed by shelter volunteers, they were more likely to have good dispositions. Lawrence had already picked one out: a fluffy black-and-white female named Mindy. I didn't care which puppy we chose—I was just ready to adopt one—so I told him to call the shelter. He did so, only to find out that Mindy had already been adopted.

That was the first of many moments when I would begrudge my husband for his inability to take action without first researching for weeks. All that work and no dog! But the woman on the phone asked if we had seen Manny. Somehow during Lawrence's extensive doggy detective work, he had not seen Manny. Of course, this made us both wonder about Manny. Was he the "so ugly, he is cute" pup? You know, the one they "forgot to put on the website"? But we agreed to have her email us a photo, and a moment later I was staring into the eyes of the most adorable puppy I had ever seen. That was it. It was love at first sight. That's the way my husband tells it.

I turned to him and pleaded like a small child. "I love him! Can we get him? Please!"

Lawrence knew he couldn't say no. Soon Manny was being shipped to us in New England from a shelter in Tennessee. As we drove to pick him up, we debated a new name for him. We rejected one after another and just could not come up with one we both liked. The CD of one of our favorite musicians, Ben Harper, was playing in the car. Suddenly it came to me: the pup was no Manny, he was a Harper! It was perfect, we both agreed.

We arrived in the pickup area at a shelter in Rhode Island and waited for our new puppy. There he was: a roly-poly little pup, all tan with a few white spots on his muzzle and front paws. He had an oddly long tail and very floppy ears, like those of a bloodhound. He was adorable. A volunteer brought him to us. Harper looked like he was content to be wrapped in the young man's arms; he was not struggling to get down at all. "This is the calmest puppy I have ever seen," the man noted.

We spent endless minutes completing paperwork, and finally the volunteer handed him over to me. Harper nuzzled right into my chest, as though he had always been with me.

We brought Harper home and in no time at all, he was into everything. He would play hard and sleep hard. This is still true of him today, at age six. Harper is long and lean like a grey-hound, and he is almost as fast as one. He has occasionally caught a chipmunk and then begrudgingly let it go when I screamed at him to drop it. After he has run around and sniffed out all possible squirrel hotspots, then barked at those he has chased up trees, he comes inside and passes out like a true hound.

Harper became my companion and partner in all activities, whether hiking, swimming, snuggling, or sleeping. At night he lay right in between Lawrence and me, which caused some re-sentment from time to time. But Harper was my baby, and there-fore he went wherever I did.

During the summers we spent many weekends in Cape Cod at the dog-friendly beaches. Harper never went in the water, but every time I would go out for a swim, Harper would follow. He would swim around me, letting the waves crash over him and paddling away. Eventually he would bump into me until I held him in the water; we called this maneuver "docking." He is a very fun, loyal, and loving dog.

As we would lie on the sand, sunning ourselves, Harper would spend the day running up and down the beach, happily chasing seabirds with his impossibly long tongue flapping away. Woe to the bird that dared to land near the shoreline. He had boundless energy! At the day's end, Harper would collapse on the couch, his head in my lap, as if to thank me for such a wonderful day.

Even after our daughter, Sophia, was born and Harper was temporarily dropped down to low dog on the totem pole, he accepted the new baby without any apparent jealousy or aggression. Our son, Ethan, was born shortly after his sister, and Harper accepted them as his pack members. Today both children are active toddlers who climb all over him, brush his coat, and dress him up in hats and tiaras. Being the good-natured hound that he is, he just lays back and takes it all in. He is completely dedicated and fiercely protective, yet gentle as a lamb around the little ones.

Harper will always be my boy, but he will also be our children's companion as they get older. I hope they will take him for long walks with friends and snuggle with him at lazy sleepovers. He will probably sleep in Sophia or Ethan's bed. He will teach them why loving animals is wonderful, and undoubtedly they will always love dogs and continue to have them in their lives— all because of Harper, our loyal, loving hound!

And okay, Lawrence, I'll admit it...I guess sometimes weeks of researching really does pay off.

Harper in the Chihuahua bed, visiting Allentown, Pennsylvania, 2006

Carl and the Gang

WHEN OUR BEAUTIFUL Pembroke Welsh corgi Rae Ann was getting older, I thought about getting another corgi puppy. They are the cutest puppies in the world—with their short legs, fat bodies, and lack of a tail, they look like little bears. Even though Rae was slowing down, I considered getting a puppy while she was still in pretty good shape. We also had our Pomeranian—Charlie—and the two dogs got along fine. I knew Charlie would be lonely without Rae. And I needed two dogs! But before I got around to looking for a corgi pup, fate intervened.

I never intended to get a Chihuahua; in fact, a Chihuahua pup would have been last on my list, mostly because they are so small and fragile. However,

I had a friend, Barb, who had bred a litter of Chihuahua puppies. She had five altogether, all males. The last I'd heard they had all been sold. But when I ran into her, she told me that there was one left—and she just happened to have the little guy with her. Barb called him Blimpo, because he was the biggest pup. He looked like a black-and-tan mouse, so I couldn't imagine how small the other puppies had been.

"The family who was going to buy him backed out," Barb told me. "Wouldn't you like a puppy?"

"No, thanks. He is just too tiny for me!" I scratched his little head. *But he was cute...* "My daughter would love to see him," I said, without thinking.

To make a long story short, we fell in love with Blimpo. He came to live with us and we called him Carl. Carl was an easy puppy. He was already paper-trained and just wanted to sit in our laps. And the three dogs got along well.

Rae passed away a few months later. And sadly, Charlie went not long after Rae. It was a terribly sad time for us. We were so happy to have our little Carl. He was very lonely when he was an only child, but that did not last long.

A week after Charlie died, Barb called me to say that she had a nice little female Chihuahua pup who needed a family. I brought her home for a trial run with Carl. At first Carl was not too happy with his new buddy, but after a while they became inseparable. We called Chihuahua number two Leeloo, after the

"Supreme Being" from the movie *The Fifth Element*.

Carl was a handsome boy. But Leeloo was a bit funny look-ing—she was rather bald and had no tail. It did not matter, be-cause we loved her so much.

It was hard to believe that I had grown into an adult who lived with Chihuahuas. I never thought I would have another Chihuahua after Piccolo. What I really could not have predicted was that I would end up living with more than two. Around this time my children went off to college and I found a new hobby. I began to help Barb with her show dogs.

One consequence of this new adventure was taking in a cou-ple more dogs. First came Jack, who failed to qualify as a show Chihuahua when he grew too big. The person who owned him was going to ship him back to his breeder in Texas—alone, in an airplane! I took him in. He was a big, goofy dog, and Carl often tried to beat him up at first. But they worked it out. Owning three dogs was a piece of cake!

Then came Gypsy, my first real show dog. She was too cute for words and took over the house. We were up to four dogs, but this was still not too bad—manageable, really.

And then came Kate, a beautiful but skittish show dog who needed some socializing. She also needed a family to love her, so I took her home with me.

Kate, I found out, was a little nuts, to say the least; she spent her first two weeks in my house hiding under the coffee table.

One of her many phobias was a fear of men. Eventually she came around and now she loves the men in the house. She started off being terrified of my son Andrew, but now she can't get enough of him. When he comes home to visit, she immediately jumps in his lap and stares at him lovingly.

It might have been wise to stop adopting dogs when I had five Chihuahuas, but that didn't happen. I added a Japanese Chin, Yoshi, whom I got from a breeder of beautiful show dogs. She was a bit crazy, but she got along with all the dogs, though she seemed to appoint herself as their leader and functioned as a benign dictator of sorts. She would not tolerate any bickering in the pack and immediately separated any violators.

Six dogs was a bit over the top for me, but they were fairly well behaved. Except for the shoe-eating phase Yoshi and Jack went through. And also the fact that Kate liked to pee on the kitchen floor when I wasn't looking.

I should have stopped there, but I had the opportunity to buy a lovely show dog from a friend when she was downsizing her kennel, so Rocky came to live with us. He was one of my favorite show dogs, and I loved him. I was a little concerned that the others would not be happy with an older dog joining the pack. However, when I brought Rocky home and set him down in the kitchen with the other dogs, they did not even notice him. It was as if he had always lived there, and we were one big happy family!

I enjoyed showing my dogs and managed to make Kate and Gypsy champions, and Rocky a grand champion. After I finished showing the girls, I had them spayed, and Yoshi as well. I wanted no part of being a breeder. I still show Rocky. He is a beautiful little dog and a joy to show. He has been very successful in the ring, and has made four appearances at the prestigious Westminster Dog Show in New York City.

My little dogs bring me so much joy. They are always so affectionate. Jim, even after so many years, still works long hours and now that our children are grown, I find myself alone a lot. But I am never lonely with my dogs around to keep me company.

So I became the crazy dog lady. Life was sometimes chaotic, but fun. "No more dogs," I said as 2010 came to an end. "I'm never getting another dog."

But then I met Bill and Ted.

Carl, as a puppy, 2007

Leeloo and Carl, 2007

Jack, as a puppy, 2008

Pretty Katie, 2009

Yoshi, as a puppy, 2009

Rocky the "rock star" with Margaret at the New York
Pet Fashion Show, 2013

The Excellent Adventures of Bill and Ted

I WAS PERFECTLY HAPPY with seven dogs. Let me rephrase that: I was happy *most* of the time. Seven dogs is a lot of work. I do not recommend owning so many unless you have enough space in your home, a big yard, and a lot of spare time and means to dedicate to their well-being. My dogs are my life. Fortunately, Chihuahuas are very small dogs who are easy to take care of.

So how did I end up with more Chihuahuas? I'm still asking myself that question.

My friend and fellow dog handler Sue decided to breed a litter of puppies. She was a good breeder and very knowledgeable, since she had worked in a vet's office for many years.

In February of 2011, four perfectly healthy pups were born, three males and one female. I came to see them, with no intention of taking any home. Not for a second did I consider another dog. *Really!* However, during my visit I realized that Sue was very attached to her little pups and did not want to sell them to anyone. This was a bit of a problem because…let's just say she had many more dogs than I did.

So one day as I was minding my own business, Sue called me and said, "Don't you want a puppy?"

"No."

"I really want you to take a puppy. I'll give you one. How about the small one? I know you really like him."

"No, thanks."

"But you are the only person I know who will give him the best home a dog could have. You will sit with him and cuddle him and—"

"*No!*" She was getting to me. I was going to lose this battle and she knew it.

"He is so small. He needs you."

"Okay! Okay! I'll think about it."

What was one more little tiny Chihuahua anyway?

I took two.

Sue had already started calling the bigger boy Bill, or Spotty Bill, because he was white and covered with tan spots. He looked like a Bill to me, so the name stuck. Bill was full of energy twenty-four hours a day, his tail always going and a toy in his mouth; he was forever bothering the other dogs. Carl kept on looking at me, as though to say, "You have got to be kidding."

The smaller dog I named Ted. Not because of any "excellent adventures," but because he reminded me of one of my son's college professors, a short redhead.

Bill grew into a beautiful Chihuahua and became quite the show dog; he is now a grand champion. After he finished his grand championship, I retired him from the ring. Bill is happier to stay home and play with Ted anyway.

Ted was not as successful as a show dog. He is tiny but has a will of iron. He wanted no part of the show ring from the very beginning! Today Bill and Ted mostly enjoy playing with the other dogs. They all love sitting and watching TV with us and getting treats, though Rocky and Bill in particular are good buddies. Tiny Ted has become quite chubby.

Bill is a dog whose tail never stops wagging. Ted just wants to cuddle. They often go to Sue's house to visit their mom, Lucy, and siblings, Tommy and Lovie. Tommy enjoys a visit from his brothers more than anything.

In 2013, Bill made an appearance at Westminster. He seemed quite bored with the whole thing and wasn't impressed with the "Big Apple" in general. Ted was happy to stay at "Aunt Sue's" house and play with Tommy. So even though Bill and Ted's adventures may not be that excellent, they always have a lot of fun, anticipating the next treat and perhaps a good belly scratch.

With the addition of the two boys, we had nine dogs, all small and still quite manageable. We continued to live in harmony, and all was well.

And then along came Penny Lane.

Bill, relaxing in the sun, 2013

Ted loves his bed! 2013

I Don't Want Any More Dogs!

LOVE ALL MY DOGS. They all get along. We have the means to take care of them. Done. End of story.

And it was, until my daughter moved in with her boyfriend in New York after graduating from college in 2011.

"We are thinking about getting a dog," she said. Margaret was home for the weekend.

I looked at her across the kitchen table. "We have a dog—several actually," I replied.

"I mean, Don wants a dog. He's never had a dog."

"You want to get a dog, *together*? Do you think that's a good idea in the city? How are you going to take care of a dog?" I shook my head. If only I'd had a crystal ball to see the future, I would have said *No! No! Absolutely not.* "Can't Don come here and just play with our dogs?" I asked.

Margaret just gave me a look.

I went on. "I don't think it's a good idea. What if you two break up? Who gets the dog? We have too many dogs in the house. No more dogs!"

"It would be his dog," she said with confidence. "If we break up, he'll take the dog. But we're not going to break up anyway." She smiled. (Famous last words...)

All I could do was weakly repeat, "I don't think it is a good idea."

A few days later, I received an excited phone call from Margaret. "We got a puppy! We named her Penny—Penny Lane!"

So much for listening to your mother. "Really? How nice. This is Don's dog, right?"

"Yes, well, she's our dog—Don's and mine. She's so cute."

"What kind of dog?"

"The shelter said she's a Chihuahua mix. She doesn't look like a Chihuahua, though—she's a big puppy."

I met Miss Penny shortly after that when Margaret and Don came to visit us. She was a leggy brindle mutt with a turned-up nose and big pointy ears. She did not look much like a Chihuahua, except for the nose and ears. She had a white chest and gray freckles. Chihuahuas don't usually come in brindle. I guessed there was some pit bull or Boston terrier in her genes, but who knew?

Penny is certainly one lucky mutt! She was born in a shelter somewhere in Tennessee. Her mother was just a puppy herself, less than a year old, when she was found on the street, quite pregnant and starving. Animal Control deposited her in the local shelter. There she gave birth to three puppies: two males and a female. One of the boys was blind. Their days were numbered because this was a kill shelter.

Fortunately, they were picked up by a foster home and the two boys were adopted together. Penny (who was named Pam at the time) was sent to be spayed along with her mom, who had been named Patsy. Pam's routine spay did not go well. She was only four months old and she did not want to wake up from anesthesia. She was pronounced dead on the operating table, but miraculously, after a few minutes, she did come around—lucky Penny Lane survived death!

Now as I look at her happily dozing in a pretty soft bed in the kitchen (*my* kitchen…), I can't help but wonder whether the surgery might have left her a little bit brain damaged. I'm mostly joking, though she certainly is goofy. But I'm getting ahead of myself.

Enter Don and Margaret. They found a listing posted by the good people who were fostering Pam on Petfinder.com, and were smitten by her big, sad eyes. They picked her up from a van full of rescued mutts, and right away they decided to call her Penny. They were told her mom, Patsy, had also been adopted. It seemed like a happy ending.

Penny went to live in the Big Apple with Don and Margaret. But it was clear from the start that she did not like the city. She was scared of everything: people, other dogs, traffic, wind, and clowns. (Just kidding about the clowns.) So she spent most of her day in their apartment.

Still, with the love of her owners, Penny was content. She learned potty training fairly quickly and was also paper-trained. She was very quiet and mostly enjoyed eviscerating toys that looked like little animals.

Her favorite thing to do with a brand new toy was to immediately rip out the squeaker that was inside. Sometimes she nibbled on the plastic so she could throw it up later. Then she pulled out all the stuffing so all that was left was a flat, noiseless carcass. This seemed to be her idea of fun!

Margaret and Don appeared to be happy, and Don did seem to love little Penny. Ah, but "happily ever after" was not to be.

Around the holidays Penny came to our house, because Don's family spent Christmas out West. Penny loved our house! We had a big yard and lots of toys to destroy. Unfortunately, the Chihuahuas never really warmed up to Penny. She never learned the art of socializing with other dogs. She meant well, but her idea of a good time was to wake a sleeping Chihuahua by pulling on its hind leg or, better yet, an ear, and then to stomp on the dog with her long skinny legs. This did not go over well with the little dogs. Penny was the country cousin everyone hid from. Her rough-and-tumble way sent all the small Chihuahuas scattering, running in all directions to seek cover.

Only Yoshi the Japanese Chin did not flee. She possessed infinite patience; maybe there's a little Zen Buddhist in her. She was also big enough (at nine pounds) to take the punishment that Penny dished out. So Penny and Yoshi would run around our house, slamming into walls and having a wonderful time while all the little dogs hid, no doubt hoping Penny would return to New York City as soon as possible.

I must say Penny was a little annoying. After she removed the squeakers from every toy in the house, one of the Chihuahuas would always find a piece of plastic to choke on. Penny also discovered that there were live toys in our big yard to chase—bunnies and squirrels! She was very good at catching them and removing their squeakers as well. But then they would not play anymore. She would nibble on them a little and sometimes show us her handiwork. She also got sick after each incident, vomiting and pooping everywhere except for outside, and always ending up at the vet's office.

Penny also learned to bark constantly at everything. Her bark was loud enough to wake the dead. And rounding out her list of charming habits was her compulsion to dig holes in the yard, into which the little dogs would always fall.

Penny was like a child with ADHD. She never napped. Never! I was not sad when she would leave after the holidays. But she was. When Margaret would get ready to go back to New York, Penny would give me the saddest dog face ever. She looked like a poster dog for the Humane Society! She loved our house—for her it was doggy "Disney World!"

And then one day, out of the blue, Margaret announced that she and Don were breaking up. Margaret promptly left her apartment (and the dog) to come home and live with us. She assumed that Don really loved Penny and would take care of her. I encouraged this belief, reminding her that "Penny was Don's dog."

After a tense phone conversation, Margaret angrily announced, "Don said he is going to take Penny to a shelter if I don't pick her up. He doesn't want her!"

"What? Seriously, he wouldn't do that, would he?" I was really shocked. I started to panic a little as I realized that Penny was about to become our dog.

"I think he's serious. He says she reminds him of us and he can't stand it."

This was not good.

And so the next day while Don was at work, we drove into Manhattan to retrieve Penny Lane and Margaret's belongings.

What a fun day that was! I'm surprised no one called the police. We parked on the sidewalk, stormed the building, and grabbed everything we could carry. We found Penny with no water, stale food, and a lot of poop on the floor. We dragged the terrified dog to the car and she sat in my lap as Margaret made an illegal U-turn onto West 95th Street heading back to Pennsylvania. Good times!

Penny had survived death and been rescued twice. Margaret eventually moved into another apartment in New York and although they never got back together, things calmed down between Don and her. He never asked about Penny.

The new apartment allowed dogs, and for a brief, glorious moment, Jim and I thought Penny might move back in with Margaret. But we knew that Penny hated the city and Margaret really did not have time to take care of a dog. So Penny stayed with us in the suburbs.

I thought Penny wanted to be with Margaret more than she wanted to be with us, until one weekend when Margaret had been home for a visit. Penny had been so happy to see her. And we felt bad when Margaret was ready to go back to New York. Margaret stood in the doorway with her coat on and a little tote bag over her arm. Penny just curled up in the bed by the door and looked heartbroken as Margaret petted her head. However, as soon as that door closed and Margaret was gone, Penny got up, wagging her tail, and dashed around the house looking for a Chihuahua to abuse. I realized she wasn't sad at all, just relieved that Margaret wasn't taking her back to the city!

Penny now lives the good life in "dog paradise" with the Chihuahuas and the Chin, Jim, and me. She sleeps in our bed, barks at the neighbors, ruins all the new toys, annoys Yoshi, and has a wonderful time. The only pleasure she is denied are her live toys, as we have squirrel- and bunny-proofed the yard.

As I write, Penny is napping along with the other dogs, weary from playing all day. She looks so sweet in the big soft bed in the kitchen not far from where I sit. She really is not so bad after all. And she just woke up to bark at something and chew on Yoshi a little. Oh well, it's just a day in the life of being one big happy family!

Miss Penny Lane, 2013

The Lovely
Miss Ella

T HERE ARE TOO MANY sad dog stories. Sometimes you have to look away, and sometimes you
just can't. It was springtime, the week before Mother's
Day, when I got the call.

"Poor Patsy. She was returned to the foster home,"
Margaret said.

"Who is Patsy?" I adjusted the phone so I could
hold it with my shoulder, trying not to drop it. I was
in the middle of making dinner for the dogs—quite a
process—and I could hardly hear her over the barking. I was always happy when she called me; usually
I just got text messages.

"Patsy is Penny's mother. I just got this long,
heart-wrenching email from the lady who runs the

pet adoptions, you know, where we got Penny."

I remembered the story of that poor dog, having been rescued from the streets somewhere in Tennessee, and I sensed that I would soon be involved.

"So what happened? I thought she had a good home."

"Well," Margaret continued, "she was adopted by this old man who wanted a lap dog, but she was scared of him and he returned her. Now they say that if they don't find a home for her soon, they will have to drop her off at a no-kill shelter where she will be left in a small cage forever. They don't think she is adoptable. She's too shy, and they have to make room for more foster dogs. That's what the email said—they wanted to know if I could take her, but I really can't take care of a dog in the apartment."

I could already see where this was going.

Margaret continued. "Now she's considered to be a 'special needs' dog. She should be with someone who has a dog, since she likes other dogs. Anyway, they are desperate to find her a home. Apparently she is very shy with people."

"Is she worse than Penny?" I asked.

"I don't know. Anyway, they said if I took her, they would waive the adoption fee, otherwise they can't keep her much longer."

"Well, maybe we can find her a home." I sighed. "I'll ask around." Being friends with a lot of people who owned dogs, I had a pretty good network of prospects to email.

"Okay, I'll tell them we are looking around and I'll send you the email and photo of her."

"Alright, I'll call you later."

I sat in front of the computer and waited for the information. The email popped up and I read the sad story of poor Patsy, rescued and then returned. (Cue the sad music.) This anonymous quote came to my mind: "Saving one dog will not change the world, but for that one dog the world will be forever changed." I was involved. The email described her as shy and plain. The photo showed her in a home full of needy dogs, and she did not stand out. Patsy was small and reddish brown, with big floppy ears. She did not look anything like her daughter, Penny.

I forwarded the email around and got two positive responses rather quickly. I was encouraged. Maybe we could find her a forever home.

And then Margaret called again. "The agency said that they would only waive the three hundred dollar fee for me," she said. Clearly they really wanted Margaret to reunite Patsy with her daughter.

"I already told people that the dog was free to a good home."

"They also said they could only keep her for another week and then she was off to the shelter. They said if we wanted her, they would bring her to a drop-off location near us."

"Okay, when do we get her?"

We could take care of her and find her a home. That was the plan.

So on a pleasant spring day, Margaret and I drove to a shopping area where a big van came to drop off dogs to their new families. There were several people waiting to receive their new pets. The large brown van pulled up, full of dogs in crates. There was a boxer, a basset hound, and a couple of mutts. The people gathered around, happily taking their dogs and paperwork as the caseworker matched pets to owners.

And then came Patsy. She looked very thin and small, and quite sad. Her eyes were blank. She appeared to be resolved to accept her fate. I knew then that she was likely to be a permanent resident at our home.

Margaret gathered Patsy in her arms. The dog was still as a rock. We drove off, and in the front seat, Margaret cuddled the little dog and petted her. Patsy relaxed a bit. I kept thinking that I couldn't have another dog, but obviously Patsy needed some loving care.

When we got home, Patsy got along fine with the other dogs. She was very quiet, and seemed grateful for a warm bed and lots of food. We renamed her Ella because she was really a pretty dog with her soft eyes, and the name seemed to suit her. The paperwork she had come with stated that she weighed eighteen pounds, but she barely weighed fourteen.

Ella and Penny got along fine, but whereas Penny was full of energy, Ella was quiet. Penny loved toys; Ella had no interest. But they both wiggled the same way when it was dinnertime, which was very cute indeed!

It just so happened that Andrew and his girlfriend were visiting us the weekend after Ella arrived, and Hannah fell head over heels in love with the dog. This was the perfect solution! Ella would find her forever home with Hannah and Andrew, and still be a part of our family.

That is exactly what happened. Ella has now gained weight and has a shiny coat to match her happy eyes. She wiggles all the time. Hannah and Andrew adore her, and she visits us often and catches up with Penny and the other dogs. She is a very well-adjusted, easy-going, and happy dog. She also likes being an only dog!

The following year, on Mother's Day, I asked Andrew if I was going to see him. He said no, that he had to take care of the dog because Hannah had plans. That let me know where I stood. I guess I'll never ask him to choose between the lovely Miss Ella and me. But seriously…the important thing is that Ella is supremely cherished, and I'm okay with that! The best Mother's Day gift for me was the privilege of knowing I have raised a son who loves and respects animals as much as I do. Who could ask for anything more?

Ella and Andrew, with Gypsy in his lap, 2013

Mother and daughter: Ella (right) and Penny, 2013

Terra

I T WAS RIGHT BEFORE CHRISTMAS of 2013 when the small white dog with black spots was surrendered to the shelter, along with a red-and-gold hand-knit blanket and a pillow. She was about ten years old, probably a Chihuahua-terrier mix with a graying muzzle and slight cataracts. They called her Terra. The woman who dropped her off said that Terra had belonged to her mother, who had passed away recently. This lady would have kept the dog, but she had fallen on hard times and had just lost her home, so she could no longer care for the animal.

The shelter placed Terra in a small cage. The place was quite noisy and she was scared and confused. Up until that point, the dog had led a good life;

her original owner had loved her. She had been happy, and was well fed and well trained. Even though this particular shelter was not a bad place—Peaceable Kingdom is a no-kill shelter with a caring staff—not many people want to take on the responsibility of adopting an older dog. So Terra languished for quite a while.

The shelter worked hard to convey her great qualities. They described her as very sweet, house-trained, good with other dogs, and content to sleep most of the time. She had no major health issues, but most people want a puppy, not a sad, old dog. To make matters worse, when people came to the shelter and approached Terra's cage, she would turn away and shake.

Eventually some people came in who wanted to adopt an "un-adoptable" dog, one who really needed a home. They took Terra, and returned her after a month. Apparently, she did not like cats and these people owned two. She also refused to walk up and down steps. Back in the shelter again, she became even more depressed, so one of the volunteers took her home as a foster care dog, which helped her perk up a bit. However, by May of 2014, she was still up for adoption and her photo was posted on the shelter website. Not one person had inquired about her.

I try to help out at the local shelter as much as I can, but I know I should not have any more dogs. It's so hard not to give in. I want to take them all. And that spring I was wavering. I thought about how the older dogs are so often overlooked, and that maybe if it was an old one, I could adopt just one more. It would have to be house-trained, get along with other dogs, and be a small breed, like a Chihuahua. Maybe I could have just one more! I knew I would take good care of another dog. I had the time, enough space, and the means to do so. And then I saw Terra.

Her story broke my heart. I asked Jim for his opinion, thinking he would provide the voice of reason. I told him her history. He immediately said, "We have to take her!" I asked one of the volunteers, a friend of mine named Heather, for her opinion, and she said it would be wonderful for Terra to be placed in our home. She wrote me a recommendation. My vet told the shelter that I got an A-plus as a doggie parent. It was a go.

And so we brought Terra home. I was worried. What if she did not get along with the other dogs? I wanted her to be happy. I could not return her to the shelter.

She came to us with her old blanket and pillow for comfort. I got her a new bed and blanket, too. In those first days, she was so frightened that she would shake when I picked her up. The first few nights I put her in her own room. She slept a lot at the beginning. I introduced her to the other dogs slowly and everything seemed to go well. Soon she had run of the house.

To make a long story short, Terra fit right in! Terra is in very good health, my vet has proclaimed. She has several good years left.

Now Terra does not sleep all day. She is quite active; she loves a walk in the park and a ride in the car. Terra still doesn't walk up the steps; in fact, she runs up and down the stairs two at time, especially when food is involved. I love to watch her little tail wag when dinner is served.

Since moving into our house, her old eyes have begun to shine. Terra loves chewies and treats, especially chicken. She even sits and waits patiently for them, unlike the other dogs in the house. Terra is very happy with her new doggie roommates. They all get along fine. And she never shakes anymore!

She is very well trained, and completely housebroken. She is very sweet and full of life, happy to be loved again. One of her favorite things to do is to sit outside in the sun. We are so glad we have Terra in our home.

If anyone out there is thinking about adopting a dog, please consider an older dog—so many senior animals need a home. An older dog in a shelter was probably loved once. They need a second chance. You won't be disappointed. Spread the word! Adopt a senior.

Terra, living the good life, Allentown, Pennsylvania, 2014

Covered in Dogs

"**I** CAN'T GET UP—I'm covered in dogs!" That is my usual response in the evening when I have settled myself in front of the TV. If anybody wants me, sorry! This is the best part of the day—the best reason to have a dog, or several. More than anything, Jim and I love to sit with the pack and watch TV and relax after work. Two laps are better than one!

Now, I don't necessarily recommend owning multiple dogs. It really requires a lot of work and dedication.

When people ask me how many dogs I have, I try to avoid answering the question. But eventually I confess. I include the fact that all the dogs are small and in total weight they add up to less than seventy-five pounds—that is hardly one medium-sized dog. I

143

mean, seriously, some people have three or four Great Danes or wolfhounds. We're talking hundreds of pounds of dog. Their poop alone weighs more than one of my dogs! And all of the dogs don't live here all the time; the kids share ownership as well.

The next question I get is: how do you manage all of them? I'll tell you about a typical day here in doggy Disney World. It begins before the sun rises, way before, at five-thirty to be exact. The first to get up is always my oldest dog, Carl.

Seven of the dogs sleep with us. The other four, who happen to be the younger dogs, like to sleep downstairs in their own room, where they each have their own fluffy bed, toys, baby blankets, and chewies. It used to be Jim's study, but not anymore. The dogs love their room, especially Ted, who sometimes does not want to come out. It is his safe place where no one can bother him, and he can be quite lazy. Terra sleeps wherever she likes; she often goes from bed to bed like Goldilocks. She has several to choose from and always finds the one that is just right!

Meanwhile, upstairs, most of the time the dogs like to sleep on or near me. Penny sleeps under the covers by Jim. Leeloo is under my arm. Gypsy is under the covers by my knees. Jack and Carl are near my. feet. Katie migrates around the whole bed. Yoshi is in between. They all snore, and so does Jim. Did I mention that I don't sleep very well?

Anyway, my morning goes like this: at around five-thirty a.m., Carl makes his way up to my head and plants his dainty paws on my neck. He then relentlessly licks my face until I peel him off. This wakes Gypsy, who nudges Carl aside so that she can also lick my face. And then Leeloo and Jack claw at me for attention as well. Jack does not lick, but he likes to sit on my chest, and because he is the largest Chihuahua, this is very uncomfortable. Yoshi and Penny then start to wrestle in bed, which they enjoy immensely!

By this time I'm up. You may ask: why don't they bother Jim? They do, but they bother me more. So downstairs I go with them to the sound of howling, because now the other dogs are up. Bill loves to howl like a wolf, as do Jack, Yoshi, and Carl. Yoshi is very musical, but Jack is quite tone deaf. Carl is a baritone. All the dogs then gather together so that I can give them a treat.

It is always still dark outside. I don't know why they get up before dawn, but by now I've realized that you can get a lot done before the sun rises, so I just go with it! At this point the dogs are very excited because they know I will reward their behavior by giving them a biscuit. After they happily eat their cookies, they promptly go back to sleep while I have my second cup of coffee. There is something wrong with this picture.

The dogs all get up again around seven, with the sun. By then, I am already showered and dressed. They go outside. I can't let them out too early because Penny barks at everything and sounds like a big Doberman—she is a very good watchdog, as long as nobody approaches her. She is actually terrified of strangers and runs away from them. But she sure sounds scary.

We have a very nice deck and yard. We had the deck extended and extra steps put in for the dogs. The yard is very large, with double fencing and beautiful landscaping. It was very expensive, but it's all for the dogs, so it was worth it.

I spend my morning cleaning—there is always a lot of cleaning. I try to keep a decent house. We even entertain sometimes, like normal people.

At eight it is breakfast time. This is very exciting for the dogs. I do this while they bark frantically as though they are starving to death. Bill claws at me and Rocky whines like a baby. Kate spins in circles while she barks, sometimes slamming into a wall. Everyone has a good time!

Of course they get expensive dog food, organic yogurt, and freshly baked chicken. (I buy five or six chickens a week, I kid you not. I tell Jim he is not allowed to eat the dogs' chicken.) I set out all the bowls and away we go. The placement of the bowls is very important; if I switch the order, the dogs get confused because each animal knows where he or she is supposed to eat.

They all eat very well...some too well. Ted looks like a little round ball with skinny legs and Gypsy has a double chin. I have them on diets, but Jim is always sneaking them extra treats.

The only ones who are picky eaters are Carl and Penny. Carl is this way because he was the first Chihuahua in the house and considers himself to be above all the others. He expects special treatment and sometimes just doesn't eat to illustrate that point. He also knows that I will hand-feed him because he has trained me to do so.

Penny, however, is a different story. She doesn't always eat because she is scared of everything. I have always fed her in a separate room so the other dogs cannot bother her. She eats slowly, unlike the others, who eat faster than the speed of light. Penny is afraid of anything different; if the room is not to her liking, she will sit on the bed and refuse to eat. For instance, if I accidentally turn on the overhead fan, forget it—she won't eat. If I move something, she won't eat. If it's noisy, she won't eat. The list goes on and on. It's a good thing she was rescued because she would not have lasted long at a shelter. I usually end up hand-feeding her, too.

The dogs spend the rest of the day playing outside, chasing each other, sleeping, and begging for treats. My home contains more toys and beds than the pet store. I take them for walks in shifts. I've tried walking some of them together, but they never seem to want to go in the same direction. Anyway, I get a lot of exercise.

People always ask me if the dogs get along. Yes, they do. They have to. I don't allow any fighting, or I should say that Yoshi doesn't. She is the pack leader and will settle any disputes by separating the parties involved. Yoshi is very serious about her job.

At dinnertime we repeat the morning procedure. After dinner, it's covered-in-dogs time for me, with lots of soft fur to pet and a wine glass in my hand.

Jim comes home and there is another lap for them. Jim likes a good martini, but so does Jack, so we have to keep an eye on him. Ted and Bill like to perch on Jim's shoulders. We relax and watch TV. The dogs doze off and we do, too.

I can't think of anywhere else I'd rather be—today and always. It doesn't get any better than this. And so from childhood to adulthood, as we watched our children grow and spent time with family and friends, our dogs have always been there for us. The world may change, but our relationships with our pets (even if they're not perfect) bring us cherished memories we'll treasure for generations. I hope to remain forever and happily "covered in dogs."

"The average dog is nicer than the average person."
—Andy Rooney

"Dogs are not our whole life,
but they make our lives whole."
—Roger A. Caras

"The better I get to know men,
the more I find myself loving dogs."
—Charles DeGaulle

"If someone tells you that you have too
many dogs, stop talking to them. You don't
need that kind of negativity in your life."
—Anonymous

"Chihuahuas are like potato chips;
you can't have just one!"
—Anonymous

(I think I may have said that one!)

 **The End**

Made in the USA
Middletown, DE
10 December 2014